Make Job Loss Work for You

Get Over It and Get Your Career Back on Track

Richard S. Deems, Ph.D.
and
Terri A. Deems, Ph.D.

America's Career Publisher

MAKE JOB LOSS WORK FOR YOU
© 2010 by Richard S. Deems and Terri A. Deems
Published by JIST Works, an imprint of JIST Publishing
7321 Shadeland Station, Suite 200
Indianapolis, IN 46256
Phone: 800-648-JIST   Fax: 877-454-7839   E-mail: info@jist.com

Visit our Web site at **www.jist.com** for information on JIST, free job search tips, tables of contents, sample pages, and ordering instructions for our many products!

See the back of this book for additional JIST titles and ordering information. Quantity discounts are available for JIST books. Please call our Sales Department at 800-648-5478 for a free catalog and more information.

Trade Product Manager: Lori Cates Hand
Interior Designer and Page Layout: Toi Davis
Cover Designer: Aleata Halbig
Proofreaders: Paula Lowell, Jeanne Clark
Indexer: Kelly D. Henthorne

Printed in the United States of America
14 13 12 11 10 09   9 8 7 6 5 4 3 2

Library of Congress Cataloging-in-Publication Data

Deems, Richard S.
  Make job loss work for you : get over it and get your career back on track /
Richard S. Deems and Terri A. Deems.
      p. cm.
  Includes index.
  ISBN 978-1-59357-740-7 (alk. paper)
  1. Unemployment--Psychological aspects. 2. Unemployed--Psychology. 3. Career development.
4. Job hunting. I. Deems, Terri A. II. Title.
  HD5708.D44 2009
  650.14--dc22

                                      2009026849

We have been careful to provide accurate information in this book, but it is possible that errors and omissions have been introduced. Please consider this in making any career plans or other important decisions. Trust your own judgment above all else and in all things.

Trademarks: All brand names and product names used in this book are trade names, service marks, trademarks, or registered trademarks of their respective owners.

ISBN 978-1-59357-740-7

Dedication

To the thousands of people with whom we've worked in JobGetting projects

And to our families for their continued support

And to Sandie, who keeps Richard grounded

And to Annie and Ben for keeping Terri on track

Contents

Acknowledgments

Many thousands of people have contributed to this book. They are the people we worked with in outplacement, career coaching, and leadership-development projects. We have learned so very much from them. Each person was a learning project, and both we and they learned—lots.

We wish we could list all who have inspired us to continue our research and application, but that would take up many, many pages. However, there are several who have greatly contributed to our success and the success of this book. The late John C. Crystal, who first developed life-work strategies, coached Richard in his early years of career management work. Crystal and Richard co-authored several articles and book chapters on career issues, and were working on three books together when Crystal suddenly died. Richard remembers what Crystal said after reviewing one manuscript: "There is too much Crystal and not enough Deems." He would be proud of this book because Crystal is there but it's a lot of Deems—and Deems.

It was in a meeting with Crystal, Roger Hiemstra, David Tiedemann, and Ginny Dennehy that Richard first heard the term "JobGetting." Someone in the group said something like "I don't care about job searching, what I care about is JobGetting!" We've used the term ever since.

Ginny Dennehy, who co-trained with Crystal, has been a major force in Richard's development as a career coach. She patiently coached him through his first workshops and provided feedback showing him how he could be among the best.

David V. Tiedemann, distinguished career education scholar, always had positive words for Richard's early work in job search strategies. Though we lost touch in later years, David gave encouragement and wise counsel when Richard needed it most.

Kathy Kolbe has helped us understand conation, the third part of the mind the ancient philosophers talked about. Her research answers the question of how we naturally get things done. It's a major component in finding that place where a person is "doing what comes naturally."

Roger Hiemstra, Richard's doctoral advisor, always encouraged him to experiment, to try out new things, and to see what might happen. Not only did Roger help Richard learn a great deal about adult development, he also introduced him to Sandie.

Other people come to mind: Ed John, who was a key staff member as our organization rapidly grew; Dick Gaither, who was always ready to sit and discuss an issue about job search techniques; Leigh Lewis, who kept us organized; Mel Rambo, CEO of Equitable Life Reserve, who eagerly followed our suggestions and helped us refine where needed; Betsy McKnight Latko, who directs our Illinois office and whose insights have added to the depth of our knowledge; Jim Luhrs, insurance CEO of our first major downsizing project, who helped us learn the importance of personal contact; and yes, Sandie, who has quietly and effectively helped us all enhance our skills as JobGetting specialists.

Read This First

If you're holding this book, and reading this page, something rather significant has happened to you. You've either been caught in a downsizing or you've decided it's time to go find the job that really fits. Either way, it's time now to dig into the work of finding, or creating, your next position.

We don't want you to just land another job, though. You can no doubt do that without any help from us, if all you want is a paycheck—any paycheck. But if you're looking for that place where you can be *fully productive* and *fully satisfied* at the same time, and want to take as little time to get there as possible, this book is for you.

As you read this, you'll see something that separates this book from others on the market. This book focuses on JobGetting, not job searching or job hunting. That's because we think your focus should be on the "getting"—not on the searching or hunting.

We've both gone through job loss and we remember what it's like. We've both set out to create jobs for ourselves. We've learned a good deal from our experience of job loss. That experience led us through more than 20 years of research and coaching people just like you through the JobGetting process. We've learned, for example, that

- **What you do in these early days of job loss will greatly influence your success in the coming weeks or months.** That's the purpose of this book: to help you deal effectively with these important first days and coach you in the direction of success.

- **There is a common pattern of perfectly normal feelings associated with job loss.** People have various reactions and emotions in response to the loss of a job. You might feel shocked, angry, or perhaps even relieved. Or you may be simply very, very confused over what to do now, or frightened about your financial future. It's very important for you to know that

  ○ These are normal feelings.

  ○ The negative feelings will subside.

  ○ There are actions you can take to make this job loss *work for you.*

- **You can make a job loss work for you!** Perhaps that's the most significant thing we've learned. You can be better off a year from now than you are today: more relaxed, more satisfied, less stressed, more productive, and more fulfilled. It will take two things from you, though: personal resolve and hard work.

Begin right now by resolving that a year from now you will want to thank the company decision makers for bringing you to this point. Then turn that resolution into reality by following our system. Sound farfetched? It's not, at least according to the people we've worked with who have used our methods. Ultimately, though, it's up to you to use the suggestions given in this book and make the job loss a move forward rather than a step backward.

If you've not already done so, browse through the contents pages. Before you go to sleep tonight, read chapter 1 on the Deems Job Loss Reaction Cycle™. Have your spouse or significant other read it with you. Then talk about it with each other. It will help put some of your reactions into perspective and help you realize that there are normal response patterns to the experience of job loss.

One More Thing

We're not denying that there can be some downer days, or that the experience of job loss is really not much fun. But this isn't the time to just sit and feel sorry for yourself or wallow in your misery. You have too many other things to do to waste time on those things.

Instead, adopt the "no sniveling" attitude, keep track of your emotions and where you are within the Deems Job Loss Reaction Cycle™, and get ready for the adventure of turning job hunting into JobGetting!

Turn the page and let's get to work!

Richard S. Deems, Ph.D.
Scottsdale, Arizona
rsdeems@worklifedesign.com

Terri A. Deems, Ph.D.
Ankeny, Iowa
tadeems@worklifedesign.com

CHAPTER 1

WHAT CAN I EXPECT NOW?

Losing a job is about much more than simply losing a job. It's also about losing important relationships, experiencing tremendous uncertainty, and even having a changed sense of self. It's an emotional experience. It's better to shed a few tears at the beginning than to pretend there's no hurt, or it doesn't bother you, or there's no embarrassment or disappointment or disorientation—only to have to deal with those feelings several months from now.

If you don't deal with those feelings now, you'll have to deal with them later, after they've had a chance to grow "underground" for a while. Worse yet, you could get stuck in one or two dimensions of what we call the Deems Job Loss Reaction Cycle™ (see figure 1.1).

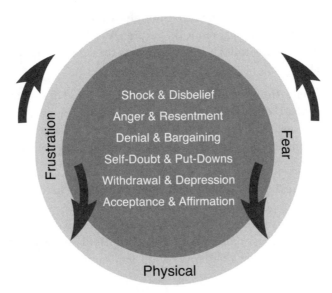

Figure 1.1: The Deems Job Loss Reaction Cycle™.

The Job Loss Cycle looks a bit like the grief cycle described by psychiatrists Westberg, Kubler-Ross, and others, doesn't it? However, in the experience of working with thousands of people who have lost their jobs, we have found that the reaction to job loss has its own unique set of characteristics:

- **First,** people move back and forth between stages, rather than moving progressively from one stage to another. That's what the arrows illustrate. Sometimes, people have reported to us, they go up and down the cycle several times in a single day. This back-and-forth movement may continue for weeks or months, and for some there are brief flashbacks to Anger and Resentment that may occur even years later.

- **Second,** we've observed that people move through the Job Loss Cycle with their own timelines. Although most experience each phase, some people remain in certain phases longer than others. Some reach Acceptance and Affirmation quickly, whereas others tend to spend a longer time in each phase. Everyone moves through the phases differently. What's important is that you don't pretend to be in Acceptance and Affirmation when you're not.

- **Third,** The Job Loss Cycle is experienced in an environment of fear, frustration, and quite often physical symptoms as well.

  - **Fear:** People tend to move through each phase with some sense of fear or uncertainty about the future. Will I find another job? How can I pay the bills? What will others think of me? How long will it take?

  - **Frustration:** People tend to experience a sense of frustration in having their lives disrupted, having routines change, having to learn new skills in JobGetting, and having to spend energy in finding a new position rather then investing energy on succeeding in an existing position.

  - **Physical symptoms:** Some people experience an increased incidence of colds and flu, and some experience more serious illnesses such as colitis, severe headaches, or ulcers. The variable seems to be the individual's ability to handle stress in efficient ways and the support that family and friends provide.

Typical Reactions to Job Loss

Within this general environment, people have the following typical reactions to job loss. These reactions are normal. Don't think something's wrong with you when you experience them. Just keep moving forward to Acceptance and Affirmation.

Shock and Disbelief

The initial reaction to job loss is a sense of shock or disbelief. After a person is told that their position no longer exists, shock, or a temporary escape from reality, takes over.

Typically, this phase takes the form of "I can't believe this is happening to me," and many people describe that they no longer hear what is being said beyond the initial announcement. People have reported that this period is "like being in a fog," and they frequently don't remember precisely what was said or done right after the announcement. They may find it difficult to perform simple tasks or to make decisions.

Shock and disbelief generally last only minutes, or sometimes hours. In rare cases, it can last for days or longer. Rest assured, this will pass. When you realize you no longer have a job, the Shock and Disbelief phase quickly moves on.

On occasion, people describe feeling shock and disbelief mixed with relief. Relief seems to come when a person has had mixed feelings about remaining in a particular position or company. Being relieved about your job loss, however, does not mean you won't experience the rest of the Job Loss Cycle.

Anger and Resentment

People tend to move quickly from Shock and Disbelief to Anger and Resentment, often within minutes. Because anger is an emotion brought about by not being in complete control of a situation, the anger is typically directed at the person(s) announcing the job loss and the organization in general.

This Anger and Resentment can come out in abusive language, pounding tables, or throwing things, and is even sometimes wrongfully taken out physically on loved ones. The Resentment dimension is often seen in an "I'll get even" kind of mindset directed toward the company and key decision makers.

Sometimes the Anger and Resentment gets turned inward, to smolder quietly. It consumes the person, who loses time thinking about "what they did to me." The person directs energy toward resentment, blame, and getting even, rather than moving on to finding that just-right new challenge. When anger gets turned inward, people tend to become sullen and move back and forth between Anger and Resentment and Withdrawal and Depression. You might have trouble identifying this while it's happening, so it can be helpful to have others around who will confront you if they see this occurring.

Many people report to us that they have experienced flashbacks of Anger and Resentment for several years after the job loss. That's not uncommon. A flashback can be brought on by a comment from someone else, or contact with someone in the past organization, or even by a quick thought that came to mind.

What can you do to constructively deal with Anger and Resentment? As with other emotions, it's important to acknowledge that it's there. Everyone experiences some anger. Even those who expressed relief at hearing the announcement nevertheless experienced anger—perhaps at the timing, which was beyond their control, perhaps simply over the way in which the announcement was made. People tell us they are able to channel this anger-energy in a positive way by focusing on their one-year goal, talking with other people about it, and finding productive, safe ways of venting when they need to.

One of the most effective ways to deal with anger is physical exercise (see chapter 2 for more about this).

Denial and Bargaining

Denial and Bargaining is a phase in which the person either denies the reality of the situation or attempts to set up various bargaining scenarios. Statements or thoughts such as "When they realize how much they need me, they'll call me back," or, "The board won't support this decision," or, "If I do this and that, they will take me back," are common.

The exact way people experience this phase varies greatly. For most, it is a very brief stage, often lasting only a few hours or a few days. For some, however, it may last for weeks. It is an escape from reality; instead of accepting the job loss, a person devotes energy to various kinds of fantasizing.

When Richard lost his job, he kept building scenarios of things he could do that would then allow his executive to keep him on. It was a futile exercise that only took energy away from his job search.

The best way to deal with this phase is to bring reality to the forefront. Did they call you yesterday to come back? No? Well, they aren't going to ask you to return. It's time to move forward.

Self-Doubt and Put-Downs

This phase may be a form of self-pity: "Look at the terrible things they've done to me." Or it could be an honest questioning of one's abilities. Either way, it can have counterproductive effects, particularly if you experience it for some length of time.

Many people begin to question their abilities after a job loss, despite a history of accomplishments. Sometimes they will even question their entire worth as a person. This questioning can lead to personal put-downs. People sometimes say to themselves, "Why did I do such a stupid thing as when I...." It only leads to more self-doubt, and the spiral continues downward.

Family members may feed into this phase more than others, knowingly or unknowingly. Because basic family relationships are impacted by a job loss, a spouse or other family member may verbally add to the self-doubt by giving out unintentional put-downs. These are often in the form of well-meaning advice or criticism, or simply asking "What did you do?" or "Why did they pick you?" Put-downs from family members only worsen the situation. This is why it is important for the whole family to be involved in learning about the Job Loss Cycle.

If you work hard at chapter 3, which guides you through identifying what you have to offer, it's difficult to remain in this phase for very long. One way to move out of this phase is to focus on what you've already accomplished in your past positions. As you focus on past accomplishments, you begin to understand that you have lots to contribute in the future. You have much to offer a new organization.

Remember, you need cheerleaders! What's a cheerleader? It's a person who knows you, wants you to succeed, and will take time to listen. It's someone who encourages you when you're down. This person won't let you sit and feel sorry for yourself. Instead, cheerleaders push and tug and remind you how you need to be out meeting people and making contacts. Cheerleaders are the people who share their energy, support, and enthusiasm so that you can turn job hunting into JobGetting. You need several cheerleaders in your life right now. Family members count, but don't limit your cheerleaders to family. You also want good friends or a supportive colleague or coach—people who speak openly and candidly and who want you to succeed.

Withdrawal and Depression

Either through a sense of embarrassment or lack of confidence, many people experience some kind of Withdrawal and Depression following a job loss. Withdrawal may range from not leaving the house to only going places where a person will not be seen by friends, acquaintances, or former colleagues. Depression comes out of a sense of having no hope.

People may also have some resistance to returning to the job market. It's as if they say "What if the same thing happens in my next job?" and so they don't try. Sometimes we see people in this phase as they resist our JobGetting strategies. When some people say "It will never work for me, so why even bother?" they are often speaking out of a sense of Withdrawal and Depression.

We've observed that sometimes the hesitancy to begin an active job search takes on many different guises. If you find yourself so busy doing yard work, painting the house, taking care of the kids, making those necessary home repairs, or spending so much time on the golf course that you haven't had time to JobGet, you may be experiencing your own form of withdrawal. You may be finding excuses not to turn job hunting into JobGetting. If that occurs, it's time to get honest with yourself.

Two things can be helpful: some kind of support system, and establishing and adhering to a daily routine or schedule. Friends and family, your cheerleaders, can provide support, or you may find it useful to join a support group or work with a career coach. And you can establish your own daily routine, which includes rising at a normal time and preparing yourself to "go to work"—except now your work is finding a new job. Remind yourself frequently that your job now is to find that place where you can be most fully productive and fully satisfied at the same time. JobGetting is a full-time job!

It's important that when you experience Withdrawal and Depression, you accept the feeling and work to turn off further put-downs. Remember, this is a normal reaction. When you experience this phase, you must be normal because this is a normal reaction. And, if you're normal, there's no real reason to stay in this phase for very long. No sniveling. There are too many other important things to do.

Here's another way people have found to help them deal with Withdrawal and Depression. The next time you wake up in the morning feeling depressed and not wanting to venture out, say to yourself, "Gee, I've earned this depression; it's normal and natural, and I am going to revel in my misery. In fact, I'm going to see how miserable I can feel, since I deserve it so very much." Then, write down on sheets of paper all the reasons to feel bad and depressed, and put those papers on the wall. Now you're ready to "celebrate" your misery. People who take this kind of an approach typically end up laughing at themselves in a short time. The depression begins to lift and the urge to withdraw begins to give way to the excitement of finding a new position.

Try it, you might like it!

> **NOTE:** Science is learning more and more about body chemistry and how we react to life events. Some people's body chemistry goes awry under stress. If you experience depression that seems to go beyond brief periods of feeling blue, please talk with your physician or another responsible specialist. It's called "taking care of yourself."

Acceptance and Affirmation

The goal! You've reached this phase when you can honestly make statements like this one:

> *I don't like it, but it has happened, and I'm going to make the most of it. In fact, I'm going to use it as a time to rethink my priorities and decide where I want to go with my future. After all, I'm a person with skills and abilities and I can make significant contributions to many different organizations.*

In other words, Acceptance and Affirmation becomes reality when a person acknowledges the situation, affirms his or her strengths, and intentionally sets about creating his or her own future. It's all about creating your own path.

Some people reach Acceptance and Affirmation quickly, and others reach it only after much time and effort. Some people may move back into one or more of the previous phases for a short time before Acceptance and Affirmation is the norm. *But it does happen!* Believing that Acceptance and Affirmation will become reality is the first step.

In fact, well over 90 percent of the people we've worked with report a year after termination, "It was one of the best things that ever happened to me. I don't necessarily want to go through it again, but I learned from it and I grew from it, and it helped me to think some things through about what's important in my life and the lives of those I care about."

Yes, you can.

Your Family's Reaction

Family members also experience the Job Loss Cycle, sometimes more intensely than for the terminated individual. The spouse is often angry because something perceived as unfair and hurtful has happened to someone very special. Family members, including children, will typically go through the various stages, which is why it is important for family members to be aware of the cycle.

Children are sometimes quiet and don't talk much about their reactions. Sometimes they are wondering, "Can I still go to college?" "What about my new uniform for soccer?" "Will we have to move?" If you have kids, stay sensitive to their moods. In general, if you have a positive attitude, so will the children.

It's also important that family members understand that this is not a time for you to do handy kinds of things around the house. They need to understand that your job is to get a new position; it is not to be a neighborhood taxi driver or sitter, or anything other than working to become a JobGetter.

We find that when family members talk openly and positively about the situation—about their anger and fears, their depression and doubt—a new bond of family begins to emerge. Family members are then able to deal with the situation out of a sense of mutual strength.

Manage Your Reactions to Job Loss

Even while you go about the basics of JobGetting, it's important that you stay aware of how you are managing the emotional side of things. Because if you don't, you could wind up taking twice as long as necessary to land that next career step.

Don't just think about it; talk about it, or write about it. What was your initial reaction when you got the word? What has it been like telling others? What fears do you have? What are you looking forward to or excited about? What are you experiencing on your best days? Your worst? What, if anything, seems to be getting in your way? Take time once a week to jot down what you are experiencing inside. This is a way to help you see just where you are in the Job Loss Cycle, and will help you remove barriers that keep you stuck.

LES'S STORY

Les was a bank executive who had worked himself up from delivery boy, just out of high school, to the number-two spot in a community bank. "It was the best job I'd ever had," Les explained, "until I was forced to move on."

One Monday morning, Les walked into his bank and into his office. But his office was bare. No desk. No photos on the wall. No chair. About that time, the new owner of the bank walked in. "Sorry Les," he began, "but I've decided to eliminate your position, so your office is now at your home." Les was stunned.

"Oh, by the way," the new owner continued, "all of your personal belongings are packed in several boxes out by the back door." The new owner briefly outlined Les's severance package and walked away, leaving one stunned 48-year-old.

Les was devastated. For the next several weeks he lounged in his pajamas all day, moving from watching TV to reading the local newspapers. His energy was gone. He stopped seeing friends. He dropped out of several community boards where he was a highly regarded member. Then he came to us.

The first thing we did was show him the Deems Job Loss Reaction Cycle™ and begin talking about what he had been experiencing. "It took me a while to move beyond Shock," Les reported. "I stayed there quite a while because I just couldn't believe it. Then the anger set in," he continued.

"My wife kept pointing out how the anger was consuming me, and then it turned to put-downs. Obviously," Les continued talking, "I must have done something really bad to be let go this way."

Our work focuses on what a person has accomplished, and we quickly moved to get Les talking about his many accomplishments—not only in growing a bank, but also in the service he rendered to his community by serving on various boards. The list was lengthy.

As we continued to focus on the Job Loss Cycle and where Les was in it, he increasingly moved to Acceptance. "What really turned me around," Les later reported, "was your challenge: Look at the current situation as opportunity and resolve that a year from that day I can go back and thank the guy who let me go."

Les's daily routine changed. He began to duplicate his earlier routine, except now he didn't go to the bank for his office. Instead, his office was in a spare room, complete with phone and computer and the files he needed. "For years," Les reported, "I would get to my office at 7:30, sit down with my coffee, and read the *Wall Street Journal*. That routine continued, except my office was now in my house. But it kept me going and a lot of progress was being made."

Les and his wife Nancy both reported that without the understanding of the Job Loss Cycle, Les would never have moved to Acceptance and Affirmation. "It's what got him off his butt," Nancy added.

A year later, Les picked up the phone in his new office and called the bank owner. "Just wanted to tell you thank you for making me get out of my rut and move forward. I now have the most exciting and rewarding job I've ever had."

JOB LOSS REACTION WORKSHEET

How have you been reacting to your job loss? What was it like when you first heard the announcement? What emotions have you been feeling since then? Write notes to yourself describing your progress and how you are moving toward Acceptance and Affirmation. Try to do this weekly as part of your reflection and goal-setting.

Some of my reactions to job loss include

_____

_____

_____

_____

_____

_____

_____

_____

_____

_____

_____

"Worry is misuse of the imagination."
—Anonymous

CHAPTER 2

WHAT DO I DO NOW?

Y ou're not alone in the process of losing a job and looking for another. Many have been where you are now and have successfully turned job hunting into JobGetting. Experience has shown there are some things you can do that will help you. And there are actions you can take that will hurt you. Focus on the Dos.

Some Dos and Don'ts

What you do in the first several days following the termination announcement often determines your success in the next several months. To help you get started, here are some specific suggestions.

Dos

These are the most important things to keep doing in terms of your mindset and relationships:

- **Think positively.** There is too much research to dismiss the power that positive thinking has on people, so think positively! Brain researcher Joseph LeDoux, in his book *Synaptic Self* (Viking, 2003), reminds us that we are what we tell ourselves. Affirm the contributions you have made in the past and the contributions you can *and will* make in the future!

- **Talk with your spouse or significant other.** Talk about the Deems Job Loss Reaction Cycle™ and where each of you is within that transition process. If you have children old enough to understand the Cycle and their reaction to your job loss, include them in conversations. Talking about it, and knowing where the other person is within the cycle, helps people move to and remain in Acceptance and Affirmation.

- **Be accessible to people.** Answer your phone, go to meetings, be ready to sit and talk. This includes being accessible to others who might be in the same situation as you. Most important, share your enthusiasm with others about using this as a chance to get to where you *really* want to be. Your enthusiasm will be contagious.

- **Continue your regular social life, community activities, and professional involvements.** People might expect you to pull back, withdraw, and be "down." Surprise them! Show them what you're made of by looking upon your job loss as an opportunity rather than as a defeat. It's important that you continue to do those things that you enjoyed and gained satisfaction from doing before the job loss.

And a Few Don'ts

Here are some things you need to work to avoid doing:

- **DON'T sell yourself short.** Okay, so you lost your job. Big deal. It has happened to millions of others in the past few years. And it will happen to many more in the next few years. Just because you lost your job doesn't mean you don't have something to offer, or that you have to take just anything in order to keep on working. The reality you want to create for yourself can't happen if you sell yourself short.

- **DON'T bad-mouth your previous employer, manager, or any other person you might hold responsible for your job loss.** People will expect you to, so don't. Why? Because if you talk only in terms of "Yes, ABC Corp. was a good company, and I made some good contributions there and I learned some good things, too..." the word will spread that you're a pretty special kind of person. After all, here you got fired and yet you're talking about how good a company it is. Don't give others a reason to wonder, "What will you say about me once we go our separate ways?"

- **DON'T sleep in.** If you start sleeping late, you'll find it very difficult to break the habit. Besides, you have too much to do to sleep in. There are phone calls to make and letters to write and people to see and doors to knock on. The more closely you continue to follow your normal schedule, the easier you will find it to make those contacts that result in job offers.

- **DON'T wait for others to contact you.** You'll find some surprises concerning your contacts. Some will contact you and offer to help in any way, and you'll be surprised because you didn't think they cared that much. Some, whom you anticipate contacting you, will not. Instead of waiting for others to contact you, if certain people are important to you, take the initiative yourself.

Now, Some More Practical Dos

If you're on the right track with your mindset, keep going with these additional Dos related to the action phase of JobGetting:

- **Keep your finances in order.** Dollars-wise, you're dealing with a lot of unknowns right now, with perhaps the biggest question being "How long before my first paycheck in my new position?" It's important to get a clear financial picture as soon as possible, and it might be necessary to cut back on spending in some areas. Whatever your financial resources, if you are going to be late in paying a bill, or need to pay less than usual, take the initiative and contact your creditor. Explain what has happened and ask what can be worked out. Because you took the initiative, most creditors will be glad to work with you.

- **Set up an "office" in your home.** Whether it's a whole room to yourself or a corner in the basement, it's important to have some specific place from which you can conduct your job search. Let family members know this is your private and personal workspace, and being in your "office" is the same as being at work. You don't need anything fancy: something to write on, a phone, some way to organize your records (box, file drawer), a comfortable chair, and space for your computer and letter-quality printer.

- **Keep in good physical condition.** If you're not doing some kind of physical activity regularly, get started immediately. It will not only help you reduce the stress and anger, but you'll feel better, have more energy, look better, think more effectively, and increase your self-confidence.

TIP: The single most effective way to maintain your energy to turn job hunting into JobGetting is physical exercise on a regular basis. This means you should be exercising at least 30 minutes three to five times a week. You can use the treadmill or stairs, run, lift weights, swim, walk, dance…just do it!

- **Plan on devoting four to eight hours a day to your job search.** That's *each* day, at least five days a week. Many people report that "there just aren't enough hours in a day to get done all that I want to get done." What are these people doing? They are following the system described later in this book. They're talking with people, researching companies, writing letters, making appointments, and meeting with potential employers. It does take time. One or two hours a day won't cut it.

- **View this as a time to decide where YOU want to be going with your life and career.** If you've not been happy or satisfied doing what you've been doing, now is the time to think through your options and design your future.

- **Accept responsibility for turning job hunting into JobGetting.** No one is more interested in your job search than you. No one other than you can do it. We can coach you, make suggestions, and prompt you on ways to most effectively present yourself. But you still have to do it. This might mean you will need to do some things that aren't easy for you. We'll talk about that later. Just be prepared to be the person who is responsible for your job search.

- **Resolve that a year from now you will thank "them" for doing you a favor!** To make that resolve a reality, however, you need to hear yourself say to others, "You know, a year from now I'll be thanking them for doing me a favor." Hear yourself saying it, and pretty soon you'll believe it. And it will become reality!

Myths and Realities

There's a lot of misinformation out there about what it takes to turn job hunting into JobGetting. Here are some of the more popular myths and what the reality is. As you will see, the reality of the job search is often different than the common myths that make up job search folklore. You need to be aware of the myths so that you can work in reality.

- **All I can do is send out a few resumes, sit back, and wait.** Just sending out resumes is the most ineffective method of job hunting. People who send out 100 resumes are fortunate if they get even four or five responses. You deserve to do better than get a mere four percent response, and we will show you ways to get a much higher response.

- **I looked through the want ads and Internet job sites, and there aren't any job openings.** Generally, only about 15 to 20 percent of the available jobs are ever listed in the want ads or Internet sites. This suggests that you should devote only 15 to 20 percent of your job search time to reviewing and chasing down want-ad information—even in online job search engines.

- **Most jobs are in large companies.** Yes, but you're looking for *job openings,* and the fact is that most job openings today are in smaller companies. You won't exclude larger organizations, but most of your job search time should be devoted to smaller companies, particularly those that are growing and need the expertise you can bring. Smaller companies are often willing to pay highly competitive wages to get the expertise they need.

- **All hiring begins at the personnel office.** Personnel offices are designed to screen you out. You want to talk with the person who has the authority to hire you, who is usually the manager or executive of the particular work area. Fortunately, it is not difficult to get to talk with that person. But you don't do it only by a letter. Get ready, because you will be making lots of phone calls. And sending e-mails. More on that later.

- **It will take one week for every thousand dollars of salary.** We consistently find no pattern for how long it will take a person to find a new job, other than this: The more hours a person spends on his or her job search each day, the less time it will take to turn job hunting into JobGetting. Those who take longest are people who have become stuck in one of the Job Loss Reaction Cycle stages or are spending only a few hours a week on their search.

- **I should take the first job that is offered.** The first job is not always the one a person really wants. The goal is to have choices so that you can choose between several offers. If you follow the suggestions outlined in this book, you can have choices.

- **I will have to take a salary cut because I'm unemployed.** No! There are so many reorganizations and downsizings going on that employers know there are a lot of very good people out there looking for a new challenge. Just because you went through job loss and are currently unemployed doesn't mean you have to take a cut in pay. What we've learned over the years is that if you were overpaid, there may need to be an adjustment. Also, when people go from one career field into another, they may need to take a temporary cut in pay. Remember that most of the people with whom we work do not take a salary cut in their next position. In fact, many people using our system end up with an increase in income!

- **Employers will not want to talk with me if they learn I've been fired.** In the past several years there have been millions of layoffs and terminations. Most have involved people with good track records and skills. Employers will think nothing of your job loss unless you call attention to it by being super-sensitive or defensive. Treat it as a normal transition in today's workplace, and decision makers will look only at your skills and what you can accomplish.

- **If they say "no," that's all I can do.** People who follow through are people who get hired. ABC Corporation doesn't have an opening for you? Fine. Ask the decision maker if she or he knows of some other company that might need someone with your skills. Ask whether you can contact the decision maker again in several weeks to see whether any new openings have occurred. Ask whether there is another unit within the company that might need someone with your skills and expertise. Those who follow through turn job hunting into JobGetting. "No" is not an option for you.

Mindset

We have a number of basic beliefs that are the foundation for this system. By reading and interacting with these beliefs, you will increase your ability to follow our suggestions because you will have a clearer understanding of why we make certain suggestions. Here are our nine key beliefs:

1. The most effective career strategy is for you to decide where you are the most productive and the most satisfied *at the same time* and then direct your energies toward that end.

2. You are truly in the driver's seat. That means you are in control. You can make decisions. You can make the kinds of decisions that get you to where you want to be, *once you have defined where you want to be.*

3. Having goals sets people free! When you have specific goals, you can direct your energies toward reaching those goals, rather than waste time worrying about where your unplanned life is dragging you.

4. People who define themselves as successful tend to have one thing in common: They have taken the time to write out their goals. Writing out a goal is making a commitment. Thinking about a goal is simply a mental exercise. There is a difference.

5. Serendipity is the experience of being on a journey to some desired goal and on that journey finding something else of equal or greater value. People who are on the journey of reaching their goals are more open to serendipity than those who are worrying about where life is taking them.

6. The decision to hire is a decision based on trust. Decision makers ask, "Can I trust this person to be what he or she claims to be? Can I trust this person to perform at the level needed? Can I simply trust this person?"

7. What you most enjoy doing is what you do best. What you do best is what you most enjoy doing. It's that simple.

8. As the late John C. Crystal used to say, "The best life and career planning is to identify what you most enjoy doing and then figure out how to get paid for it."

9. To be successful, focus on what you most enjoy doing, and then do it—very well!

MINDSET WORKSHEET

This is the kind of mindset I'll use:

_____

_____

_____

_____

_____

_____

_____

These are steps I'll take to maintain my energy and mindset:

_____

_____

_____

_____

_____

_____

_____

SHARON'S STORY

Sharon's employer had been experiencing the results of the economic downturn. And with declining business, there wasn't the need for as many people in the accounting unit. She knew this, and it was no surprise when she and a few others were told of their layoff. As she was clearing her personal items out of her desk, she thought about the others who were also involved in the layoff.

The next day Sharon called the others to find out how they were coming along with the reading their job counselor had given them and if they had read the section on the Job Loss Cycle. Several of the people she called were people she had supervised, and one person was even her old boss. They agreed to get together in the next week.

Sharon got to work. She cleaned out a space in the spare bedroom and even took down the bed so she could have more room. She moved in a desk, phone, computer, printer, and file boxes. She was ready.

One of the first things she did was to make a poster to put on her wall—nothing fancy, just a piece of cardboard. She used colored markers to highlight her phrase: "A year from now I will thank them!" She put her poster on the wall where she would see it every morning when she went to her "office."

Then she started the task of identifying what she did best and what she had to offer a new employer.

That night at the dinner table she explained to her family that her job now was to get a new job. She would be spending several hours each day turning job hunting into JobGetting. The family spent some time talking about the Job Loss Cycle and where each person was within it. Sharon encouraged everyone to move to Acceptance as quickly as possible. Although it was not fun, she asked her family to look at her job loss like she was: as the opportunity to find a great place where she could be most fully productive and most satisfied at the same time.

They talked about finances, and how, until Sharon had a new job, some things would need to be cut back. The vacation? Time would tell. After dinner Sharon and her husband looked over bills and credit cards and made some decisions about things that could be postponed. They started to work on a realistic budget.

Before the layoff, Sharon would run each morning. She kept that up, and even increased how long she was running. Later she added weight training at a local fitness center. People remarked about how energized she looked.

It took Sharon four months to find that "just-right" job. She found it, the way most people find a new position: through networking. And yes, she got a pay increase. During those four months, she grew in self-confidence and in feeling in control of her life. She had set her sights on a specific kind of new job and stayed with it until it was hers.

"It was telling me that I was going to make this work that made the difference," Sharon said after beginning her new position. "And I kept telling myself that I have lots to contribute—and I do."

"The future depends on what we do in the present."
—Gandhi

CHAPTER 3

WHAT DO I HAVE TO OFFER?

Before you can turn job hunting into JobGetting, you need to describe what you have to offer a new organization—you know, the things you've accomplished in past jobs that you can accomplish in a new position. The results of your work. Why is it important? Because past performance is the best predictor of future performance. If the results of your past work have been very positive, decision makers will want you on their team. First, however, you need to take the time to identify the results of your work.

This activity is not an option; it's a basic requirement to turn job hunting into JobGetting. You will identify what you have to offer by taking a hard look at what you've done before. Then you spend some time thinking about the best way to describe what you have to offer a new organization.

The extra time you spend now identifying and describing the results of your work will make it easier later. You'll be better prepared to

- Write a resume that gets results
- Describe to decision makers what you can do for them
- Write cover letters that get results
- Maintain your confidence and energy to find that right spot for you
- Turn job hunting into JobGetting

Here's how you do it:

1. First you'll list the tasks, functions, projects, and responsibilities of past positions, giving the most attention to the most recent years.

2. For each item you've identified, you will ask yourself "So what?"

3. You'll push yourself to see whether you can quantify the results of your work, and begin to prepare one-liners.

4. As you review all that you've accomplished, you'll start looking for patterns. We call them "personal themes" and we're convinced we all have them.

5. Finally, you will come up with a page that describes you: what you've done, what you've been recognized for, what you've accomplished, and what you most enjoy about your work.

The result will be a clear description of what you've accomplished and a list of action statements with quantified results. You will use this information as you explore your options, develop your resume, and begin to practice talking about what you have to offer.

Step 1: List Tasks, Functions, and Responsibilities

The first step is to make a complete list of the tasks, functions, and responsibilities of your previous positions. This becomes your working database of experience and strengths. You will devote more time and energy to analyzing the past 5 to 10 years of your work. Don't, however, exclude significant results from previous jobs.

Copy the following worksheet for each of the job titles you've had, even jobs within the same organization. For each job, list in as much detail as possible what you did in that job: the tasks and functions you performed and the responsibilities that were yours. Make each page as comprehensive as possible. The more information you generate, the less chance there is of forgetting something important.

JOB RESPONSIBILITY WORKSHEET

Job title: _____

Company name: _____

Location: _____

Start date: _____ End date: _____

Tasks, functions, and responsibilities: _____

_____

_____

_____

_____

```
_____

_____

_____

_____
```

Here are two examples to help you understand the kind of information you need to be gleaning from your career history:

Example #1

Vice President, Industrial Group Operations, XYZ
Manufacturing, Columbus, Ohio, 2008–present

- Asked team to look at ways to cut costs.

- Managed startup of new processing and packaging plant.

- Led marketing team to increase sales.

- Initiated new inventory-control practices.

- Reduced customer backorders.

- Examined food packaging options.

- Held P&L responsibility for manufacturing locations.

- Managed new capital projects.

- Initiated concept of self-directed teams.

Example #2

IT Manager, ABC Insurance Company, Neenah, Wisconsin, 2009–present

- Developed systems for tracking information about new insurers.

- Directed team to redo company website.

- Coordinated preparation of department's first long-range strategic plan.

- Prepared company's annual report.

- Explored investment accounting and reporting system.

- Directed team to recommend new software and hardware for underwriting department.

With your lists complete, you are ready for Step 2.

Step 2: Ask "So What?"

For each task, function, or responsibility identified, ask the question "so what?" What happened because this was part of your job? What happened because you did some specific activity, managed some project, or initiated some new way of doing things? Ask yourself, "What happened because I did that?"

Here's how the "so what?" question works. Let's take the last item from Example 1, "Initiated concept of self-directed teams."

Ask, "So what?" Well, you formed teams based on who had the right natural strengths.

So what?

Well you trained the teams in how to be self-directed.

So what?

Well, you had to spend less time supervising the self-directed teams than other teams.

So what?

You had more time to devote to other teams and you realized that fewer people left (turnover) self-directed teams than other teams.

So what?

You do some math and realize that your turnover in self-directed teams was reduced by 60 percent.

So what?

You can do some more math and figure how much in dollars you saved the company by reducing turnover. And by reducing turnover, you no doubt also increased productivity of self-directed teams.

You are trying to get at the results of your work so that you can talk with decision makers about what you can contribute in their organizations. You know you can make these contributions because of what you've contributed in the past.

Here are several "so what?"s from the preceding examples:

Example #1

- Team identified six ways to reduce costs.
- Managed startup of a new processing and packaging plant and increased production.
- Handled design, construction, and regulatory at same time.
- Helped company grow from a regional producer to a national competitor.
- Reduced inventories and saved time and dollars.
- Reduced customer backorders and increased customer satisfaction.
- Established new industry standards for food packaging. New plastic packaging seen as industry leader.
- P&L responsibility for 6 manufacturing locations.
- Reduced turnover in self-directed teams.

Example #2

- Implemented systems to track new insurers to retain their business.
- Revised company website and increased daily hits.
- Team produced first long-range plan for department with specific goals and objectives.
- Received several awards for company's annual report.
- Installed the first PC-based investment accounting and reporting system. Reduced operating costs and cut time to prepare reports.
- Increased financial flexibility by revising $15M in short-term and long-term investment portfolios.
- Designed and implemented new underwriting systems. Doubled underwriting transactions with only 3 new staff.

You can take the "so what?"s another step to provide even more detailed information about what you can contribute to a new organization based on what you've done in the past. Read on.

Step 3: Quantify Results and Prepare One-Liners

Next, go back through your tasks, functions, and responsibilities with your "so what?" notes and quantify your results. For example, if you reduced turnaround time, by how much? And once you've calculated by how much you reduced turnaround time, you can calculate increased customer satisfaction, reduction of costs, and so on. If you increased accuracy or efficiency, by how much? If you reduced turnover, by how much? And how much did it save the company? And by how much did it improve performance?

Don't be concerned about absolute accuracy; estimate the results as close as you can. This doesn't mean you have license to lie, but don't refuse to identify a specific result because you "just aren't sure." If you're plus or minus a few percentage points, that's close enough. If you're not sure whether you saved $10,000 or $12,000 each month, use whichever figure is the most comfortable for you.

Perhaps you think that what you did can't be defined in terms of numbers. In that case, think of other results your work might have had: higher customer satisfaction (can be measured), ensuring that regulations are met (can also be measured), or the office operated smoothly (higher efficiency can be measured). As you realized, you can quantify each of those preceding examples with either a dollar sign ($), percentage (%), or number (#).

Wait, you're still not done. For each of your pages, copy the following worksheet and use it to go back and rewrite your results' lists into one-line statements. Begin each statement with an action word. Appendix A contains a list of action words you can use. Here are some brief examples of one-liners.

ONE-LINER WORKSHEET

Job title: _____

Results one-liners:

_____

_____

_____

_____

_____

_____

_____

One-Liner Examples from #1

- Reduced labor costs by 23% and scrap loss by 28% through implementing cost-control techniques.

- Directed startup of $15M food processing and packaging plant and expanded production by more than 35%.

- Increased market penetration by 31% through development and implementation of new functional, user-friendly plastic packaging, which remains the industry standard.

One-Liner Examples from #2

- Increased first-year customer retention from 53% to more than 85%.

- Received five national awards for producing company's annual report.

- Increased number of underwriting transactions by 50% with addition of only 3 new staff.

Now you're ready to take yet a different look at what you have to offer.

People who look at resumes are used to seeing what we call fluff—you know, statements like these:

- Managed a cost-cutting team.

- Identified ways to increase first-year customer retention.

- Developed new strategic plan.

Nice statements. But they don't tell us much about what the writer did. People who interview you will want to know the results of your work; what you accomplished; with numbers, dollars, or percentages. Taking extra time now will make it easier later to prepare your resume. And you will have important information to share with decision makers about why you're the right person for the job. You will read more about one-liners in chapter 5.

Step 4: Identify Your Major Themes

We believe that everyone has several major themes. These are the things a person has consistently done well over the years—and enjoyed doing. For example, one of Richard's major themes is helping adults become more self-directed. One of Terri's major themes is helping adults move more easily through life changes. As both of us look at our lives, we realize this is what we've been doing throughout our careers, even though we did those things in several different settings. Terri never had a formal job title of "helper of adults moving through life changes." At this point, job titles don't mean much. Your concern is to identify your personal themes.

Review all of your results-oriented lists, looking for the major themes of your own personal strengths. These are broad categories into which you can place most of your previous one-liner statements. Keep analyzing until you can identify no more than three major areas. These key strengths are skills areas, not qualities. What's the difference? Skills have to do with things you can get accomplished, whereas qualities relate to how you govern yourself.

Skills Include Things Like	Qualities Include Things Like
Managing people	Self-motivated
Organizing operations	Honest
Leading project teams	Dependable

Your personal qualities will show through in the interview process. For now, however, the emphasis is on *skills* and *what you can accomplish* for someone else.

Why should you narrow it down to just three? People reading your resume or listening to you describe what you are able to do for them can remember three areas of expertise (strengths) much more easily than they can recall five.

Here are examples from our earlier lists:

Example #1

Startup plant operations

Packaging innovations

Cost-containment strategies

Example #2

Business communications

Accounting systems

PC-based operations

After you've reviewed your lists of one-liners, identify your three skill areas and write them in the following space.

MY THREE MAJOR THEMES

My major areas of strength include

1. _____

_____

_____

2. _____

_____

_____

3. _____

_____

_____

Step 5: Describe Yourself

The final step is to develop a page describing yourself and the results of your work. The one-liner statements you've developed will be the basis for your resume. And they will help you think through your options in chapter 4. If you can put these statements into three major categories, that's great.

The final sentence in your description begins with the word, "Enjoy…" and states what you most enjoy doing in your work. Take time to think this through. You want that final sentence to clearly summarize what you most enjoy doing in your work. The interviewer will probably notice your statement and discuss it during your interview.

Think first of a label—such as *Plant Manager, Sales and Marketing Director, Lead Accountant,* or *IT Supervisor*—that summarizes your efforts and accomplishments. Here are two brief examples. Your summary will be much longer.

Product Operations and Marketing Executive

Commended for ability to effectively lead production efforts.

Increased market share from 3% to more than 40% in less than 8 years. P&L responsibility for manufacturing operations exceeding $55M. Recognized as an innovator and turnaround specialist.

Enjoy the challenge of finding new ways to get things done that reduce costs, enhance product, and increase revenues.

Chief Financial Officer

Developed system to increase cash-management yield by more than 17%.

Increased department efficiency by more than 20% through implementing new PC-based accounting systems.

Commended for ability to effectively work with state and federal regulators.

Simplified financial reports and recognized by Investor Relations committee for "plain talk."

Developed new reporting materials to increase the readability of complex concepts and information.

Streamlined accounting functions with increased efficiencies of more than 23%.

Enjoy tackling complex treasury and accounting problems and finding solutions that work.

Now, in the following space, write your own "What I Have to Offer" paragraph describing all that you've accomplished. Try hard to come up with the three major categories (your major themes, from step 4) and then appropriately place each of your one-liners under one of those categories. Be sure to include as your last statement a well-constructed sentence describing what you most enjoy doing.

WHAT I HAVE TO OFFER

Major Theme #1

One-liner descriptions:

_____

_____

_____

_____

Major Theme #2

One-liner descriptions:

_____

_____

_____

_____

Major Theme #3

One-liner descriptions:

_____

_____

_____

_____

PAM'S STORY

When Pam was told she was one of six whose jobs were eliminated, she wasn't surprised. Her recent assignments didn't call for what she most enjoyed doing and she had already been looking for another position. Her position as the coordinator of on-board training involved a lot of detail and record-keeping—more than she enjoyed.

One section in the job-transition workbook she had been given caught her attention. It focused on strengths—on identifying what one does best because that's what one enjoys doing the most. She understood the concept. She made her lists of tasks and responsibilities, asked "So what?" for each item, and was able to quantify just about everything on the list.

She realized her personal themes all dealt with learning. She could identify learning needs, design learning projects, and conduct learning programs. Then she started putting her one-liners into one of those three categories:

- Identify learning needs:

    ○ Review production records and identify learning needs.

    ○ Assist in performance-review sessions to identify employee learning needs.

And she kept on going. Then she turned to her second category.

- Design learning projects:

    ○ Designed more than 15 learning modules to increase performance.

    ○ Designed on-board learning project that reduced time for new employees to learn accounting system by more than 15%.

And she added more statements.

- Conduct learning programs

    ○ Consistently receive Very Good to Excellent ratings from more than 90% of workshop participants.

    ○ Conducted more than 36 learning programs in past fiscal year.

And yes, she added more statements—and results.

As Pam looked over her notes, she began to realize that there were some items listed that she really didn't enjoy doing. So she scratched them. The idea, she had learned, is to focus on what a person most enjoys doing because that's what a person typically does best. She deleted those past results that didn't fit with what she most enjoyed doing. She still had a long list of past accomplishments.

And what did she most enjoy doing? "What I most enjoy doing," Pam wrote, "is to help adults learn what they've identified they need to learn." Pam continued until the page was full. She placed one-liners under one of the three categories. She used numbers, percentages, and dollar amounts as she described what she had accomplished in past jobs.

Now she was ready to focus on her options.

"The best life/career planning is to identify what you most enjoy doing...and then figure out how to get paid for it!"
—John C. Crystal

CHAPTER 4

WHAT ARE MY OPTIONS?

You have options. Everybody has options. And you're not limited to just one or two jobs. To identify your top options, you will need to think in terms of the three parts of the mind:

- Thinking (cognitive)
- Feeling (affective)
- Doing (conative)

To put it another way, your options are based on your best skills and experience (cognitive); your values, temperament, and what's important to you (affective); and your natural strengths (conative).

As you work at identifying your options, you'll discover an interesting phenomenon: When you realize you have options, you can truly evaluate where you've been. Maybe you really enjoyed what you did before, and maybe not. Some who have taken time to evaluate where they've been have said, "No way, I want something different." Others have said, "I enjoyed it and want something similar." And still others have reported, "I liked what I did, but I sure want a different kind of work environment."

This chapter shows you how to identify your best options.

Taking Stock of Yourself

First, get a handle on what you have to offer an employer and what you want: special knowledge and content skills; your values, feelings, and what's important to you; and your natural strengths.

Special Knowledge and Content Skills

Review the results of your work from chapter 3. As you review what you have to offer, think in terms of your special knowledge and experience. What have you learned through formal education, on-the-job experience, and your own reading and asking questions? What do you use in your work that came from formal education or training courses? What do you use in your job that came from experience—from "learning the hard way"?

Think about the content knowledge and information you have and that *you enjoy working with.* This special knowledge can come from specialized training, your own learning projects, or from having done a certain set of things for a length of time. For example, we've worked with people who had special knowledge about a variety of topics, including

Financial lending	Loan applications	Marketing
Spices	Soaps	Compensation
Career design	Direct sales	Segment marketing
Public relations	Telemarketing	Managing others
TV production	Plant operations	Adult learning
Wastewater management	Cookbook design	Cement production

Okay, that's enough; you get the idea. Everyone has some of these cognitive specialties, which they've developed by working in their fields for some time. In the following worksheet, describe the special knowledge and information skills you have, *and identify which ones you prefer to continue using.*

KNOWLEDGE AND INFORMATION SKILLS WORKSHEET

My special knowledge and content skills include

_____

_____

_____

_____

_____

_____

_____

_____

_____

_____

_____

_____

_____

_____

_____

_____

_____

This is a description of your cognitive strengths, the personal strengths that come from learning and experience. This represents the *thinking* part of your mind.

Values, Feelings, and What's Important to You

Next, take some time to reflect on your values and what's important to you (the affective part of your mind). There are a number of very good affective assessments, such as the Myers-Briggs Type Indicator (MBTI). The MBTI measures your temperament: the way you respond to external events and stimuli. It is a kind of personality test. There are other personality tests, which identify and describe social styles. There are also value indicators, which identify your particular value-set.

One way to examine your values and feelings (your affective strengths) is to make a list of people you admire. These can be people who are alive or deceased; people you've met or people you've never personally known; people who are famous and people who aren't known outside their community. Here's an example of how your list might look:

Howard Deems (dad)

Sam Deems (grandfather)

Abraham Lincoln

Aunt Marian (my aunt)

Barack Obama

Virginia Dennehy

PEOPLE I ADMIRE

_____

_____

_____

_____

_____

_____

_____

_____

_____

_____

After you've identified a number of people you admire, go back over your list. For each person, write what you admire about that person. Don't worry if you admire the same thing in more than one person. That happens. Just make your list as complete as possible.

Take another look at it. Now you have more insight into your values and what you consider to be important—the affective part of your mind. Your values impact the kind of organization you want to be part of, as well as the work environment. Your values also impact on what motivates you.

Affective assessments don't tell you how you naturally get things done (conative) or what your IQ is (cognitive). But they are helpful in clarifying what's important to you, what your values are, and how you want to relate to others. All of these factors play into defining your ideal job.

The affective part of the mind is dynamic; that is, it's always changing. So you may value one thing one year, only to find you value something different a year later. Why does it change? Because it's a value, a perceived "want," and it has to do with the affective part of a person's mind. And it's an important part of the mind to think about when trying to identify your options.

Take some time to think about yourself and your temperament. Are you an introvert or an extrovert? Are you gregarious or shy? To get you started thinking about your temperament, think in terms of the following:

- **Introvert:** Gains strength and energizes from within; from solitude; by being quiet, alone, reading, listening to music, thinking....

- **Extrovert:** Gains strength and energizes from being around people, talking with others, doing things with others, being part of a group....

Within both the Introvert and Extrovert ways of being, a person may also be either shy or gregarious:

- **Shy:** Less at ease in the company of others; tends to be more quiet. May hesitate to meet strangers, doesn't find it easy to meet new people, takes time to get acquainted with people....

- **Gregarious:** Outgoing, forward, even boisterous; easily meets new people and welcomes the chance to make friends out of strangers, easily talks with anyone....

Where would you place yourself? Why?

Think also about *personal qualities* you have, such as "highly motivated," or "dependable," or "stick-with-it-until-it's-done," or "driver," or "follower," or (you insert the word). And what motivates you to do something, instead of nothing? Is it money? Prestige? Comforts? Recognition? Saving the environment? Contributing to the greater community? Family? Job well done? Or something else?

Now put it all together into a brief paragraph. Here's an example:

High energy, likes to be in charge, usually a gregarious extrovert, likes to be part of a collaborative team but also wants the opportunity to handle projects by himself, welcomes feedback from others, wants to set his own schedule, motivated to do his best when given the go-ahead, needs to try different approaches to get things done, likes to write, wants to contribute, likes recognition.

Okay, you get the idea. Now integrate your information and thoughts into a description of your temperament and personal qualities, the affective part of your mind.

TEMPERAMENT AND PERSONAL QUALITIES STATEMENT

My temperament and personal qualities include

_____

_____

_____

_____

_____

_____

_____

_____

_____

_____

_____

_____

_____

_____

_____

_____

Natural Strengths

Now we turn to the conative part of your mind, your natural strengths. These strengths are the way you naturally make decisions, solve problems, strive toward your goals, and in general get things done when you're free to be yourself.

Conation might be a new term for you as the third part of the mind the ancient philosophers talked about: thinking, feeling, doing. Conation (doing) is being studied more and more in the U.S., although the concept has been studied in other parts of the world for years.

Here's one way to understand conation. You can *think* about a possible solution to a problem and come up with a plan (cognitive). You can *believe* in the plan and *feel* that it is a good plan and you *want to make it happen* (affective). It is only when you *act,* you *carry out the plan,* that anything gets done (conative).

We all know that actions speak louder than words, but it wasn't until the cutting-edge work of management specialist Kathy Kolbe that a valid instrument existed to identify and measure a person's conative strengths. Kolbe identified four Action Modes®, which she calls Fact Finder, Follow Thru, Quick Start, and Implementor. These modes have to do with how people initiate action, not how they think or how they feel.

Fact Finder refers to the instinctive way we gather and share information; Follow Thru is the instinctive way we arrange and design; Quick Start is the instinctive way we deal with risk and uncertainty; and Implementor (think of a farm implement) is the instinctive way we handle space and tangibles. The Kolbe A™ Index identifies a person's strength on a 10-point continuum in each of the Action Modes, identifying a person's natural need to initiate action, respond to needs, or prevent problems in each of the four modes.

Kolbe has identified 12 methods of problem solving, also called Kolbe Strengths™. Although we can all solve problems using any of the 12 methods, each of us has four (one in each Action Mode) that allow us to do our best.

Figure 4.1 illustrates the four Action Modes and 12 methods of problem solving.

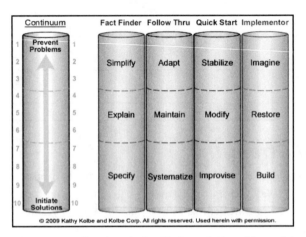

© 2009 Kathy Kolbe and Kolbe Corp. All rights reserved. Used herein with permission.

Figure 4.1: Kolbe's four Action Modes and 12 problem-solving methods.

We do our best when we tackle challenges in ways that are most natural for us.

Nobody is at the 7-8-9-10 end of the continuum in all four Action Modes. No one is at the 1-2-3 end of the continuum in all four Action Modes, either. One person may problem solve by Explaining, Adapting, Improvising, and Restoring. Another person may problem solve by Specifying, Maintaining, Stabilizing, and Imagining.

We use Kolbe's insights into behavior because in her paradigm there are no "shoulds" and no weaknesses. It is not better to be in the high range in any one mode, and one method of getting things done is not better than another. As illustrated in figure 4.1, there are only strengths. Industrial psychologist Veronica Schmidt Harvey said, "It is all so very positive! There are no 'shoulds' in this system!"

Take time to look at the conative strengths and where you might fit. Only the Kolbe A™ Index, however, can identify your true conative strengths. Although we can't reproduce the Index here in this work, we believe it is important enough to bring to your attention. Here's why. When you have a position that calls upon your natural strengths (conative strengths), you are the most effective, productive, and satisfied. The opposite is true, too.

A person who is in the 7-8-9-10 range in Quick Start *needs* to take risks, *needs* to try new things, and *needs* to improvise solutions. It is not a *want* (affective), but a *need* (conative). A person who is in the Initiate range in Quick Start will not do well in a highly structured position where there is no opportunity for improvising, risk, or the freedom to try out possibilities.

A person who is in the 7-8-9-10 range in Fact Finder needs to be in a position where he or she can examine specifics, gather information on what has and has not worked before, and determine the best approach before making the final decision or recommendation.

A person who initiates in Follow Thru is a natural organizer, someone who can easily (naturally) systematize, put things in order, and plan what needs to happen first, and then second, and so on until a project is finished. This person needs to finish what they start and bring closure to each task before starting a new task.

A person who initiates in Implementor (physical energy) needs to work with his or her hands or with tools. This person needs to be able to physically "show" what he or she has accomplished. Place an initiating Implementor in a job that requires the person to sit behind a desk all day without access to the outdoors, whether it is a window view or physically going outside, and that person will become stressed.

To be highly effective, people need jobs that call upon their natural, conative strengths. Take time to go back to figure 4.1 and identify what you believe is your strength within each of the four modes.

In the worksheet that follows, briefly describe what you think are your natural strengths.

NATURAL STRENGTHS WORKSHEET

My natural strengths and instincts include

Fact Finder = _____

_____

_____

(continued)

(*continued*)

Follow Thru = _____

_____

_____

Quick Start = _____

_____

_____

Implementor = _____

_____

_____

Putting It All Together

Review your "What I Have to Offer" statement from chapter 3. Integrate that statement with the information from the worksheets you've completed so far in this chapter. Now you can write a paragraph that describes you and what you do best, which is the same as what you most like to do. Here's an example:

> Gregarious extrovert who enjoys and excels at meeting new people, needs to experiment and try out new things, and has the following best skills:
>
> • Leading others through developing the vision, and enlisting the support of others to reach the vision.
>
> • Putting together and leading teams that work well and get things done.
>
> • Evaluating plans to identify the components that will bring the vision to reality.
>
> I enjoy doing these things in a service-industry setting, and I know a great deal about insurance and how to organize people and work to get things done.

Use this as a guide and an example as you write your own summary statement.

Putting It All Together: My Summary Statement

_____

_____

_____

_____

_____

_____

_____

_____

_____

_____

_____

_____

_____

_____

_____

_____

_____

_____

_____

Your Ideal Work Environment

Now it is time to think about the kind of work environment that best fits you. If you have to work, it only makes sense that you work in the kind of environment in which you can be fully satisfied and fully productive at the same time. Otherwise, why bother?

Most of us have worked in that kind of environment at one time or another. Think back through your career history. In what job, or at what times in several jobs, were you both fully productive and satisfied at the same time? What position or parts of positions energized you, left you feeling good at the end of the day, or made you eager to get up in the morning and get to work? What was fun?

Maybe you can't think of a time related to your career history. In that case, think of non-work times you felt this way. What were you doing? Where were you? Who were you with? What was the environment like? The point is to try to identify the essence of such experiences or environments, and to use these insights in your JobGetting.

Now, with these positions in mind (your most enjoyed job or jobs), describe the following in as much detail as possible:

- What the setting was like, including the physical setting and work climate

- The kinds of people with whom you worked or interacted

- How you were supervised

- What your typical schedule of activity was like

- What you were doing, your actions, and what your duties or responsibilities were

- What other things made that environment so satisfying and productive for you

Now put it together into a statement about your ideal work environment.

MY IDEAL WORK ENVIRONMENT

_____

_____

_____

_____

_____

_____

_____

_____

_____

_____

_____

_____

_____

_____

_____

_____

_____

_____

_____

_____

_____

_____

_____

Top Job Options

Now it's time to take what you know about yourself and use it to identify your top job options. Look over everything you've written in this chapter. Take another look at chapter 3 and the summary you created on page 31. Think about what your best options seem to be. Focus on the duties and responsibilities, not necessarily the titles, at this point. If you know what these jobs are called, add the titles. Keep in mind the insights or descriptions you wrote about in the other steps.

Fill in these blanks to guide your thinking:

My ideal job calls upon me to use my skills in…

Working with people who…

And the physical environment features…

And… (something special you'd also like if you can have it).

Here's an example:

My ideal job calls upon me to use my skills in organizing people, stream-lining procedures, and finding new ways to get things done; working with people who are energetic, competent, and willing to work hard; in a facility that has lots of windows with sleek, modern furniture; where I can set my own schedule.

Here's another example:

My ideal job calls upon me to use my skills in problem solving, identifying plausible options, and leading a team to follow the most useful option; with people who care about what they do, who like to be "the best," and who share many of my own values; in a green facility that's within easy driving distance of my home.

Take time now to write your own example of your ultimate job:

DESCRIPTION OF MY IDEAL JOB

My ideal job calls on me to use my skills in…

_____

_____

Working with people who…

_____

_____

And the physical environment features...

_____

_____

_____

And... (something special you'd also like if you can have it)

_____

_____

_____

_____

_____

_____

_____

_____

_____

If you don't know what this job is called, or if you'd really like this kind of job even though you've never had a job like it before, go to pages 52–55. Take time to read about exploring your options. Some call it field surveying. Some call it information gathering. It is a proven way to explore options and try on a job even before you've ever had that kind of job.

Here's still another way to list your options. Fill out the following worksheet, listing duties and responsibilities, possible titles, companies that might hire someone like that, and who you know who might know someone who needs a person for that kind of job.

Option #1

Primary duties and responsibilities:

_____

_____

_____

Possible title(s):

_____

Companies that hire such people:

_____

_____

_____

Contacts I have who might help:

_____

_____

_____

_____

_____

Option #2

Primary duties and responsibilities:

_____

_____

_____

Possible title(s):

_____

Companies that hire such people:

_____

_____

_____

Contacts I have who might help:

_____

_____

_____

Option #3

Primary duties and responsibilities:

_____

_____

_____

Possible title(s):

_____

Companies that hire such people:

_____

_____

_____

Contacts I have who might help:

_____

_____

(continued)

(continued)

Option #4

Primary duties and responsibilities:

_____

_____

_____

_____

Possible title(s):

_____

Companies that hire such people:

_____

_____

_____

Contacts I have who might help:

_____

_____

_____

_____

Exploring Your Career Options

Okay, so you've identified your major accomplishments, categorized them into three strengths, and described the things you like best. But you've never had that kind of job before and you don't really know if you'd like it. There are a few good ways to find out.

Informational Interviewing

The late John C. Crystal used to call it field surveying. Others call it information gathering or informational interviewing. It makes no difference what you call it. Here is how it works.

You can get started in one of two ways. Let's say you have identified what you do best and most enjoy doing. But you don't know what that kind of job is called. Now's the time to return to your networking friends. Contact them again and tell them, "I've identified the three major things I want to be doing in my next job. Do you know what such a job is called, or do you know of someone who might know?" Then continue networking until you find some people who are ready to talk with you.

You can also talk with HR managers of area companies. When you call for an appointment, tell them you've identified what you do best, but you don't know what the job titles are for people who do those kinds of things. Listen to their responses. Take notes. And then ask for the names of people who have the kind of job you *think* you want.

Contact these people and ask for a time when you can meet and talk with them about what they do. Tell them you've been doing some career exploration and one of your top options is a position similar to what that person is doing. But before you jump, you want to learn as much as you can about what it's really like to do that job.

Arrange for a meeting and be ready. Your first question is, "It will help me if you can tell me what you *like most* about your job." Listen carefully. As the person describes what she or he likes best, ask yourself, "Would I like doing that?" You will no doubt have follow-up questions such as "I don't understand what you mean by...and it will help me if you can explain it in more detail."

After you've exhausted that topic, be ready with your next question. "It will help me if you can explain what you *like least* about your job." Listen carefully. Would you dislike it also? Or maybe you find yourself thinking, "Gee, too bad the person dislikes that, because I think I'd like doing that." Again, there will be more detail questions.

Now you know what *one person* likes and dislikes about the job you're considering as your goal. Hint: If the person can only talk about what he or she *dislikes* about the job, make a note. That position will probably be open in the next several months.

You need one more bit of information: "It will help me if you can tell me what it takes to get into this kind of position." Again, listen carefully. When they are finished, you will know what special education, experience, or licenses you need to get that kind of job.

Before you leave, be sure you have the person's name, title, address, phone number, and e-mail address. As you get ready to leave, you can say something like this:

> *This has really been helpful to me and I appreciate your time. I'd like to explore this further. Who else do you know who does something similar? And can you give me the person's name and contact information? And may I use your name when I contact that person?*

Send a thank-you letter the next day expressing your appreciation for the person taking time out of his or her busy schedule to share information with you. This person is now part of your network. You will contact the person again when you've decided your direction and are ready to do your networking.

Sometimes the person you are talking with gets so excited talking about what he or she does, and is so impressed that you had the genius to talk with them about it (remember, a person's favorite topic of conservation is what that person does), they might tell you they'd like to hire you—now.

But you were not out there looking for a job. You were wanting information. Tell them thank you and explain that you're still exploring. If working in that organization is really what you want, add one more statement:

> *I appreciate your offer, but I'm just gathering information. Let me think about this some more and if I believe there is a fit, let me contact you in a day or two.*

And then, if you're really interested, contact that person again after several days. Tell him or her that you've had some time to think about it, and yes, you'd like to talk in more detail about what the person is thinking and where you might best fit.

How many people do you need to talk with before making a decision? It depends. You need to gather enough information so that you can say you either do or do not want that kind of a position. But always talk to more than just one person.

Either way, when you reach your decision, you have a network of people you can use later to help you find the opening that has your name on it.

Ask Other People the Three Questions

A very effective way to explore options and find out what's out there is to simply ask others the three questions. When you're at a neighborhood gathering, talk with others about what they do. People are always glad to talk about what they do. And if you show a genuine interest, you have just invited a person to talk about his or her favorite topic. If you ask Rhea what she does, she will be more than glad to talk about her favorite topics: herself and her work. People are always glad to talk about what they do.

Go ahead and ask the three questions: What do you like best about your job? What do you like least? What does it take to get into this line of work? If you want to explore further, ask the next question: Who else do you know who does this kind of work—and can you give me his or her name and contact information—and can I use your name?

After you talk with each person about what the person does, be sure to send these people a thank-you note. They are now part of your network and you will want to contact them again in the near future. For more about that, refer to chapter 7.

Remember, you have options. We all have options. Your task is to identify your best options and then figure out how to get hired.

NAM'S STORY

Nam was six when his parents moved him to the United States. He went to public schools, spent two years at a community college, and then earned a degree in business from a state university. He found himself working in claims within an insurance company. Although he liked parts of the job, he wasn't fully satisfied.

When Nam was told that his job was one of quite a few being eliminated, he was really down—for a few days. Then he began to realize that this could be the time to think through, as an adult, what he really wanted to do. First he assessed his knowledge and special experiences. He began to appreciate that he knew a lot about insurance. It was a field that, for some reason, interested him. He could tell you all about what it takes to make an insurance company successful. This was his special knowledge.

As he continued to assess his strengths, he turned to what others had said about him. "You're a hard worker, a driver," others had frequently said. And he knew it was true. He wanted to be in charge and he wanted to lead. It was easy for him to meet people and put them at ease, and co-workers said he was really enjoyable to work with. These were his affective strengths.

(continued)

(continued)

Nam not only liked to learn, he needed to learn: new things, what worked before and what didn't work before, and research. He needed to solve problems and deal with specifics. As he explored his natural strengths, he acknowledged that he wasn't a risk-taker. He worked best, he said, when he had an assignment and knew what he needed to get accomplished, and when. These were his conative strengths.

Nam started to put it all together, describing in more detail his cognitive, affective, and conative strengths. He knew he wanted to be somewhere in the insurance field. But he didn't want to sell. And he didn't want to do claims. Instead, he was drawn toward solving problems. Nam's conclusion? He now works as a risk specialist within a medium-sized insurance agency. He researches potential clients and identifies their various risks and the kind of coverage that best fits their needs. Then he makes his recommendations.

Nam loves it.

AL'S STORY

Al had been a tire builder for a number of years. It was an okay job and paid well. He wasn't particularly disappointed, though, when his plant was closed.

Al went through the processes in this book. In talking with friends one night, a neighbor suggested he look into insurance underwriting. Al headed to the library, asked where the insurance periodical section was, and started reading. What he read caught his attention, even though he couldn't fully explain why. He picked up two textbooks on underwriting and headed home.

His neighbor knew a couple of insurance underwriters and gave Al their names and phone numbers. Al set up a meeting with each of them. For each meeting he was ready with three basic questions:

- What do you like best about your job?

- What do you like least about you job?

- What does it take to get a job like this?

As Al listened to each underwriter describe what he or she liked best and least about the job, Al was thinking: Would I enjoy doing that?

Would I not like doing that? He listened carefully about what it takes to get a job as an underwriter.

Al talked with enough underwriters about what they did that he knew what underwriting involved. And he liked what he heard. Al decided underwriting was his job objective. As he was out networking one day, a friend said, "Hey, yesterday an underwriter's position just opened up. Let me take you down the hall and introduce you to the unit manager."

The meeting went well and Al decided to apply for the job. After he was offered the position, he asked about his competition. One person who had been interviewed was just out of college with a degree in insurance, and the other person was already an underwriter in another company. But Al seemed to know more about underwriting than the other two because of all his research. And he had more enthusiasm. He has done very well as an underwriter. And he really enjoys it.

> "To be successful, focus on what you most
> enjoy doing and then do it very well!"
> —R.S. Deems

CHAPTER 5

WHAT ABOUT A RESUME?

Do you need a resume? Yes!
Will it get you a job? No!

Maybe it will get you an introduction—maybe not. But it can, and does, serve as a reminder to decision makers of who you are and what you have to offer. This means you need to spend a significant amount of time on your resume to make it the strongest, most strategic document possible.

Resume Basics

Let's first put the resume in perspective. Your resume is a "word picture" of you: the positions you've held, the results of your work, your educational achievements, and perhaps even some of your non-work activities. Sometimes, the resume is the first introduction an employer will have to you. You will want it to have a positive impact. Other times, the resume will be a reminder of who you are and what you have done after you've talked with decision makers.

Here are a few basic ideas to keep in mind:

- A resume does *not* get you a job. *You* get the job, following a face-to-face interview. A resume may or may not get you an interview.

- *Never* lie on a resume! This will only create problems for you later and can be a reason to fire you after you've been hired.

- Take the time and energy to think about the best way to present yourself, and select the right words to describe what you have accomplished.

- Keep in mind *who* will read your resume and what you want them to know about you. You don't need to put down everything. But you will need to show that you have a history of getting things done and that you're ready to continue that tradition.

- Your resume might not look like others you've seen. That's okay. The recommendations we offer in this book are based on what decision makers tell us they like to see and what candidates tell us they get the most positive reactions from.

You will probably get lots of advice from other people about what your resume should look like. Thank the people for their concern and interest in your future, because that does mean a lot. Chances are, though, these people are simply telling you what they're used to seeing, or what they prefer to see. You want to focus on what hiring managers say about resumes, and that's what this chapter is all about.

There is simply no single best way to construct a resume today other than the tried-and-true rule of "no fluff." What works best for you may not work as well for someone else, and vice versa. What is important is that you consider what you need to get across to a decision maker and the best way to get that done.

Resume Layout and Format

You developed much of the material for your resume already when you completed chapter 3. Now it's time to pull together that material in a way that will present the clearest, strongest picture of you.

When it comes to format, there are several options concerning length, style, and layout. Whether you are doing a first-time-ever resume, or have one that you simply want to punch up a bit for your JobGetting, consider these questions.

How Long Should My Resume Be?

The quick answer is, "long enough": long enough to show a decision maker what you have accomplished in the past and what sets you apart from other qualified candidates.

For someone just out of school or seeking an entry-level position, a one-page resume might do the trick. It's not likely to be adequate, though, for someone with several years of successful work experience.

For someone seeking a faculty position at a university, a six-page curriculum vitae might be in order, but that six-pager will not work for a mid-level manager in a for-profit company.

What decision makers tell us is this: "Give us enough information so that we know who you are and what you've done, so we can form an opinion on what you can do for us…just don't give us any fluff." For most people, a resume of one to four pages will work, and two pages is most common. A three-page resume is most common for executive levels. Just be sure you make good use of the space you have. Know your targeted market well enough to know what is likely to make the most positive first impression.

The longer resumes are less of a concern today than they once were because of the use of electronic submissions. Still, you don't want to give decision makers a small book to read, because they're not likely to read it. Consider your reader's interests and needs, along with the information you most need to convey. Then create a resume that is indeed "long enough" and that invites someone to read it. Depending on the particular kinds of positions you are exploring, you may end up with several different resume versions, each of different lengths.

TIP: One layout style we've found works very well for the longer hard-copy resume is a portfolio resume: a single piece of 11 × 17–inch paper, folded in the middle. Although it has four pages for copy, it is often considered a one-pager because it is only one physical piece of paper.

What Format Should I Use?

There are two basic resume formats. A *chronological* format lists your positions and descriptions of accomplishments in reverse-chronological order (the most recent job first), and is considered the more traditional format for a resume.

A *functional* resume puts the emphasis on skills and major strengths. Usually three (and not more than five) major strength areas are listed, with specific examples of accomplishments to illustrate each strength. Following this description of strengths is a work history section that includes a chronological listing of positions, often with three-to-five one-liners describing the results of your work. Check out the examples in figures 5.1 and 5.2 to see how each of these might look.

David J. Jasperson
5529 Meadowlark Dr.
Lancaster, Arkansas 72200
444-490-4121
djj571@msn.com

Career Summary

IT Manager with more than 10 years of experience managing IT functions within a financial institution setting. Directed up to 30 programmers and systems analysts, with operating budgets exceeding $3.5M. Involved in numerous conversions, consistently bringing projects in on time and below budget. Commended by end-users for "ability to come up with the right solutions for the real problems." Recognized for staying current with new technologies and drawing on this knowledge to find innovative solutions to performance problems. Enjoy a fast-paced environment, new challenges, and the opportunity for continuous improvement.

Major Strengths & Accomplishments

- *Project Management:* Develop high-performance teams that create innovative and practical solutions to end-users' problems, on or ahead of schedule.
- *Financial Management:* Skilled in developing accurate budgets and financial projections, and in administering budgets for highest efficiency.
- *Reorganizations:* Increase productivity and profitability through assessment of a department's strengths and weaknesses, change planning, and implementing the hard decisions necessary to enhance performance.

Career History

Director, MIS Services, JD Brothers, Inc., 2005–present. Direct MIS functions for 900-employee financial services institution with 13 branch locations. Examples of accomplishments include
- Reduced overhead by 17% through consolidating and upgrading various data-processing functions.
- Increased productivity by 21% through implementation of Performance Review system, which focused on incentives for reaching productivity goals.
- Created project team to systematically evaluate services and promote continuous improvement efforts.
- Led cross-functional team to assess needs, evaluate options, and select and develop a corporate learning management system that resulted in 31% reduction in training costs.

Manager, Help Desk Services, ABC Corporation, 2002–2005. Managed 13 programmers and analysts to customize applications for up to 22 departments. Accomplishments included
- Implemented 24/7 telephone support to increase accessibility to users for both routine and non-routine questions.
- Designed basic configuration and led installation of key security software.
- Recruited, hired, and trained 5 new staff members to expand technical capacity.

InstaMark, St. Clair, WI, 1997–2002. Promoted through positions of increasing responsibility with Fortune 500 company. Accomplishments included

Help Desk Supervisor (2001–2002)
- Supervised staff of 7 help desk technicians to resolve common user questions.
- Managed internet accounts for employees, including setting up and closing accounts as needed.
- Installed peripheral equipment, including printers, mice, and keyboards, and resolved common issues.
- Trained new employees on intranet system.

Figure 5.1: Chronological resume example.

David J. Jasperson
djj571@msn.com

InstaMark, continued

Help Desk Technician (1997–2001)
- Installed software and provided user support for Windows and Adobe applications.
- Assisted in diagnosing wireless and Ethernet network problems.
- Installed new software and updated software as needed to resolve spyware and virus issues.

Additional employment includes programming (1996–1998) for family-owned business while completing degree work.

Education & Training

Master of Science in Business Administration
University of Nebraska–Lincoln, 1998
Thesis: "Effects of Selected Software on Productivity"

Bachelor of Science
ITT Technical Institute, Omaha, NE, 1996
Major: Computer Engineering

Continuing professional education includes participation in numerous courses, seminars, and company-sponsored workshops, including network systems, Web design, and technical project management for e-commerce.

Professional & Community Activities

- **President, Association for Information Systems** (local chapter), 2008–present; board member, 2005–2007; member, 2000–present.
- **Member, Administrative Management Society,** 1998–present.
- **Task Force, Metro Chamber of Commerce:** Chaired committee that prepared Blue Ribbon Technical Report for Governor's Office.
- Active in local church.

What Others Say

- "A real team player—keeps people working well together."
- "Sticks with it until the problem gets solved."
- "I've always enjoyed working with Dave, whatever the project."
- "He knows how to work well with a wide variety of people."
- "Dave has a knack for leading others and making sure his people feel like a valuable part of his team."

The more common format is the chronological, which lists specific results under specific job titles. This format often works best if you are making a move within a single industry or seeking a position similar to one you held before.

If, however, you are making a significant career change—changing fields, for example, or seeking a position that in some other way is quite different from what you have done before—the functional format may work best. The functional format provides a way of highlighting those experiences that will be most important in your new job, and takes the focus off previous job titles or industries. A functional format also gives you more flexibility for using your resume in different ways.

For many people in the midst of JobGetting, we suggest a combination of the chronological and functional formats. This is a modified chronological or modified functional format. This quickly shows decision makers the themes or areas of strength you bring, yet also provides a chronological listing of positions you've held.

Regardless of the format you choose (and many people develop one resume using each format, for maximum flexibility), keep in mind what you want to accomplish with your resume: a clear picture of your strengths and where and how you can make contributions. You want to make it as easy as possible for the reader to see how you bring the strengths they need.

Cindy Hernandez

1552 E St. NW
Washington, DC 20006
(202) 123-4567
chz76@gmail.com

Career Summary

Human Resources Specialist with more than 6 years of experience in various human resource roles to effectively support corporate objectives. Extremely effective in problem-solving and conflict resolution. Recognized for generalist HR background. Frequently requested by supervisors and managers to assist in resolving performance problems. Able to successfully manage a wide range of HR issues. Enjoy showing people how to be their best.

Experience includes

Employee Relations	Compensation	Recruitment
Policy Application	Staff Development	HRIS Database
Management Consulting	Benefits Administration	Budget Management
Employee Activities Planning	Employee Orientation	Distance Learning

Examples of Accomplishments

❏ *Employee Relations*
- Increased company score on employee attitude survey by more than 10 points through development of new performance system.
- Commended by senior managers for ability to coach supervisors on effective employee relations in areas of supervision, discipline, discharge, motivation, and performance-evaluation procedures.
- Commended for work in the culture transition of a major marketing company to a world-class organization.
- Participated in the assessment of corporate communications; coordinated and proctored corporate employee survey resulting in 98% participation.
- Assisted in planning and implementation of two major downsizings involving more than 450 exempt and non-exempt employees with zero litigation.

❏ *HR Policy & Benefits Administration*
- Ensured management practices were consistent with all federal, state, and local employment regulations.
- Reduced EEO and Affirmative Action inquiries by more than 38% through supervisor training and coaching.
- Administered/coordinated compensation and benefits programs for more than 600 employees; gathered survey information, processed benefits enrollment information, responded to questions, resolved problems, and ensured necessary documentation was provided to corporate office.
- Participated in 30 unemployment hearings resulting in 100% favorable rulings.
- Maintained payroll information and prepared all required standard and ad hoc reports.
- Served as point of contact for benefits questions for more than 1,000 employees; coordinated and troubleshot employee benefits and Workers' Compensation issues.
- Coordinated and completed benefit/employment documentation related to data center and production elimination.

(continued)

Figure 5.2: Functional resume example.

(continued)

Cindy Hernandez, chz76@gmail.com, Page Two

Examples of Accomplishments, continued

☐ *Staff Hiring & Development*
- Managed and participated in the planning, sourcing, recruiting, testing, and screening of more than 500 candidates for employment.
- Hired more than 100 non-exempt employees with retention exceeding 85%.
- Commended by managers for assistance in identifying staffing needs, procedures, interviewing techniques, compensation, and employment legislation impacting recruitment practices.
- Surveyed management to identify critical training needs and designed/conducted more than 25 training sessions.
- Coordinated speakers and training programs, and facilitated training in areas of employment documentation and company culture.
- Implemented new software for successful tracking of more than 800 applicants.

Career History

AMC Projects, Washington DC, 2007 to present
Human Resources Manager, 2009–present
Assistant Human Resources Manager, 2007–2008

FAB TechTronix Corporation, Roughneck, Colorado, 2004–2007
Recruiter, 2005–2006
Human Resources Administrative Assistant, 2004–2005

Additional experience includes *Personnel/Administration Coordinator* and *Personnel Counselor,* 2002–2004

Educational Background

Bachelor of Science in Business Administration
Boston College, 2001
- Emphasis in Human Resource Management
- Active in intramural sports
- Self-funded 90% of all educational costs

Professional and Community Activities

Member, Virginia SHRM; Member, Delaware Small Business Association; Active in local church, local and state politics

What Others Say

- "Cindy is a delight to work with and can disagree without being disagreeable!"
- "When I needed some help in dealing with a disciplinary issue, Cindy was willing to listen, and without being judgmental provided some very workable suggestions."
- "As CEO I don't usually have people argue with me in staff meetings—but Cindy did, and she was right! Thank you."
- "Always a good listener."
- "Cindy's command of what good human resource management is, is outstanding."

What Kind of Paper Should I Use?

Although many people send their resume electronically—either for convenience or at the request of a decision maker—there are bound to be times when you simply want a nice hard copy to hand out to people when making an application or introducing yourself. The paper you choose can help make a positive or negative impression on the reader, just as other design factors will.

Use a paper that you personally like, because this is one more piece of information that tells a decision maker something about who you are. Or you can think about the reader or the organization. For example, if you know an organization makes use of many "green" practices, using a good recycled resume paper would be smart.

TIP: If you are seeking a position within a more creative field, let your resume show some of your own unique creativity or personality. Create a logo for yourself, a unique watermark, or some other design element that helps convey a sense of who you are.

Resume Content

Although the layout and design elements of a resume can help you make a strong first impression, it's the content that will really grab a reader's attention. This section discusses the major parts you'll want to include in your resume.

Heading or Banner

At the top of the first page, centered, put your name, address, a daytime telephone number, and e-mail address. If you are still working but cannot be contacted at your office, use your home phone number or your cell phone.

TIP: Be sure you have an answering machine or voice-mail system with a professional-sounding greeting. This isn't the time for something clever or silly.

Although there are other banner designs that you can use, we like the simple, centered format because it has a clean look to it and fits well with almost any resume format you decide to use. Use a slightly larger font size in the banner, and use bold on your name. (You want people to remember your name!) On your contact numbers, there is no need to use words such as "telephone" or "e-mail" because any reader will be able to recognize what they are.

Career Summary

Next comes your career summary, professional profile, or whatever you choose to call it. Do *not* use an objective. Decision makers tell us the objective is not a helpful statement and just wastes valuable space. Be careful, because many resume-builder software programs continue to prompt you to include this. The career summary is more helpful because it gives readers a quick overview of who you are, helps them understand your major strengths, and encourages them to read the remainder of the resume in more detail.

The career summary or profile can be compared to your reply to the interview question, "How would you describe yourself?" The paragraph you developed in chapter 3 (Step 5: "Describe Yourself") is a good beginning statement. Your summary should be a concise statement, five to seven sentences long, providing a quick overview of your major strengths and accomplishments. For example:

> *Customer Service/Call Center Manager* with more than 11 years of experience in sales, handling customer inquiries, and resolving complaints. Demonstrated success in leading departments with up to 30 sales staff. Expertise includes hiring, retaining, and developing a committed workforce; managing multiple priorities; and using new technologies to enhance service. Recognized for ability to build productive teams and reduce costs. Enjoy a fast-paced environment that values the highest quality of performance.

> *Manufacturing executive* with 15 years of experience directing production, marketing and sales, and new product development. Recognized as an industry innovator in packaging and identifying new products. Commended for reorganization of production operations, which reduced overhead by 17% and improved quality of products. Elected president of international industry association. Enjoy finding solutions to complex product-to-consumer problems.

> *"Front office" professional* with associate degree in office management and 5 years of experience in healthcare clinic settings. Skilled in making patients feel welcome and comfortable. Experienced with standard office equipment and MS Office software, including Excel and Word. Detail-oriented; effectively handle multiple priorities and enhance existing systems and procedures. Excellent communication and interpersonal skills. Enjoy helping people feel comfortable in the clinic environment.

Note that the summary, like the rest of the resume, is written with an "assumed I." For example *{I am} Recognized for...* and *{I} Enjoy....* Do not write your resume as if you were writing about another person; it's all about you! You do not, however, need to use "I" in your description.

Because you want each resume to be targeted for the particular position you are seeking, you can write this summary differently for different positions. So think it through. Consider what might be most important to the reader and what keywords they may be looking for, and work those into your description. Just make sure, of course, that what you say is truly an accurate picture of yourself.

We suggest you end your summary with a sentence that begins, "Enjoy...." This last sentence should be a summary of what you most enjoy doing, which is also what you do best.

Key Strengths

Beneath your summary or profile, you add a brief section that lists your major strengths or areas of expertise. These represent qualifications you want to highlight. Like the summary, this section may change depending on the particular position you are applying for. If you are submitting your resume online, this could also be a keyword list, to help make it easier for people to find you in a resume database.

Just as you did with your summary, think about what the reader is likely to be most interested in seeing, and provide that. For example, if the position requires someone with a particular kind of content, equipment, or mechanical knowledge, list or describe those that you have.

Depending on your abilities and the needs of the position, your key strengths, areas of expertise, or examples of expertise might look like this:

- Sales & marketing
- Project management
- Hiring & retaining the best people

Or it might look like this:

- Preventive maintenance
- Transmission & drive train
- Diesel service
- Routine inspection & computerized diagnostics
- A/C service & repair

For a longer list of major strengths, create a two- or three-column listing, as this person uses for his teaching content areas:

- Creative Writing
- Speech & Debate
- Am. Literature
- Composition
- Language Arts
- Poetry
- Critical Thinking
- Drama
- Grammar & Basic Skills

Sometimes it's appropriate to even add just a small bit of description:

- Training & Development: Designed, developed, and delivered formal learning events involving up to 250 learners.

- Distance Learning: Use eLearning and mLearning technologies to deliver learning programs and events.

- Needs Assessment & Evaluation: Ensure appropriateness of training through careful analysis of needs, and verify learning transfer through multiple levels of evaluation.

The point is this: You want to clearly direct the reader to your skills or knowledge areas and make it easy to see the strengths you have. And you want to do this in about the first half of the first page. If you can't capture a decision maker's interest by then, it's not likely that the person will read the second half of the page. Your "piece of paper" will be added to the pile of other ho-hum resumes.

TIP: When listing skill or content areas in a single column, use an odd number of bullets; for some reason, people tend to respond more positively to an odd number of bulleted items than to an even number.

Work History and Action Statements

Now you're ready to get even more specific by providing your work history or background. The way you set this up varies depending on whether you are writing a chronological resume or a functional resume.

For Chronological Resumes

You'll have a separate entry for each position you've held, with a focus generally on the past 10 years. On one or two lines, put your job title, the name of the organization, the city and state where you worked, and the years you worked there (no need to list months). You can boldface this line and use italics for the job title.

An old format for this section is to use two columns, but we'd suggest you not do this. It uses up valuable space and makes the readers focus on a title or a date, rather than on what you accomplished. Remember, you want to help the reader see what you contributed, not simply what title you held or the dates you worked.

Under each job title, include a listing of one-liner action statements, describing the results of your work. Remember how, in chapter 3, you wrote your tasks, functions, and responsibilities and then quantified the results? This information will provide the basis for your action statements.

A list of action words, like that found in appendix B, can help you find the right word to begin each one-liner. You can also find many good lists of action words online. Brief, bulleted, one-sentence statements are the most effective because they get right to the point and are easy to read. The emphasis should be on the *results* you produced in your previous positions so that decision makers can see what you can produce for them. Remember: *Most other candidates looking at the same position you are will have similar skills as you.* What will set you apart are your accomplishments and specific contributions.

Be specific. What was the size of the budget you directed? How many people were in your work group? If you developed a new system to improve efficiency or accuracy, how much time was saved? If you saved the department money, how much? Identify how the results were achieved. If errors were reduced by 10 percent, what did you do to achieve those results? If you're not sure about a particular number, you can say something like "Reduced errors by approximately...." Be sure to include special recognition or commendations you've received; your resume is not the place to be modest.

If you have many years of experience, you may be wondering just how far back to go. A decision maker will usually focus on the most recent experience you've had, and that's where you want to provide the most detail. As a general rule, list specific positions going back 10 or so years. If you have a longer work history, you can also list it but not provide as much detail, or even any bullet points at all. As with any rule, however, there are exceptions. For example, perhaps something in your more distant past is very relevant to the position you are now going after, and more recent work is not. In that case, you might provide more detail from the past or consider using the functional resume format.

For Functional and Combination Resumes

If you are using a functional format or a combination format, you might take out the key strengths section and instead create resume subsections around those areas of strength. Then, within each of these subsections, you will group your one-liners under the appropriate headings.

For example, perhaps you have identified three key strengths: *Retail Sales, Customer Service*, and *Promotions & Marketing*. Below your career summary, you will create a section named, for instance, Examples of Accomplishments. Under this main heading, you can do something like this:

Retail Sales:

- Selected as Salesperson of the Year for 3 consecutive years, with sales consistently 22% higher than other sales staff.

- Engage customers to learn more of their personal interests and needs, and direct them to most appropriate products to enhance sales.

- Trained new sales staff on store protocols.

- Assisted store buyer with product selection and purchasing.

Promotions & Marketing:

- Developed store marketing campaigns with holiday themes, resulting in our store achieving highest sales volume within our chain.

- Maintained Web site with special online promotions to increase online sales as well as foot traffic.

- Used variety of software programs to create flyers and newspaper advertisements.

Customer Service:

- Supervised a team of 8 tasked with responding to customer complaints.

- Received at least 5 letters of "thanks" from customers served.

- Frequently asked by other supervisors to assist in training employees to effectively deal with angry customers.

Following these action statements, you will also want to include a Work History section. Here, you will list your job titles, organizations, city/state, and annual dates, along with a brief, one- to two-line description of your primary job responsibilities.

Education

Education will come near the end of your resume. If you are a recent college graduate, it's more appropriate to put the Education section toward the beginning. If you are preparing a curriculum vitae, put the Education section after your career summary. Include *only* your post–high school studies. List your formal educational achievements in reverse-chronological order, with the most recent first. Identify your college or university, the year graduated, the degree earned, and your major course of study if appropriate for the job you are pursuing. For example:

> Bachelor of Science in Business Administration
>
> University of Hard Knocks, Boondocks, California, 2009
>
> Minor: Psychology

If you graduated in the past one to three years, you might also want to include your GPA (if it's high) or other academic awards and activities. And if you took particular courses or engaged in research that is very relevant to your career direction, you might also want to include this information as well.

In addition to your degree(s), also include other professional development activities you have taken part in, especially if they included licensure or certification of any kind. Your goal here is to indicate that you've continued your education beyond the classroom. Be sure to include specialized training you might have received during your previous employment.

No Formal Degree

What if you do not have a formal degree but did attend a college or university for a time? Go ahead and show the school, the years attended, and your major course of study:

> University of Hard Knocks, Boondocks, CA, 2009
> - Completed 32 hours in Business Administration program.

Did Not Attend College

What if you did not attend college? Do not indicate graduation from a high school. Generally your reader will assume that you did. Instead, you might name this section Training & Professional Development instead of Education. Then, think about what training events you have taken part in: workshops, seminars, training events at previous workplaces, and so on. List these by name, or give a more generic description, such as this:

> Professional development has included taking part in a variety of training events including MS Word 2007, conflict management, communication skills, negotiation, and team building.

If you cannot think of anything to list here, simply skip this section of your resume.

Professional and Community Activities

Decision makers like to see people who are involved in professional or community activities. List the professional associations you are involved in or community activities in which you participate, particularly if you held any type of leadership position. You might also include memberships or activities that you no longer do, if they were fairly recent and relevant.

If your activities include specific religious or political affiliations, do not specify what they were. Instead, make a statement such as "Active in neighborhood church" or "Participated in political campaign activities."

Endorsements

There's one more section we like to see on resumes. We call it "What Others Say." This is a listing of three to five quotes of what others have said about you. These endorsements may come from performance reviews; thank-you notes; good things your boss, peers, or subordinates have said to you; or even positive comments that customers have said to you. Think of these as "mini-references" (remember, JobGetting is no time to be bashful).

Decision makers often tell us that this is an unexpected part of the resume. But they like it! It is a way to convey a bit more of your personality (not an easy task in a resume); it helps to support what you've said in other parts of your resume; and it can present a picture of your strengths that may be difficult to capture in other sections.

Take some time to think about this. What positive things have others said about you? Look at past performance reviews. Dig out those old thank-you notes you've saved. Read through the letter of reference someone wrote for you. Or just think about those "hallway" remarks we all get from time to time. Some people create a master list of such comments and keep it in their personal file (if you don't have one of these, start one in your new position); then they pull out the most relevant quotes when it's time for JobGetting.

Your endorsements might look like some of these:

> "Great job on that Jamison project—your energy and innovative ideas were critical in getting the job done!"

> "Terri, you are awesome! I've learned so much from you!"

> "There is absolutely no mountain too high for Jose to climb!"

> "Your positive spirit and endless energy have made all the difference around here. I couldn't ask for a more supportive supervisor!"

> "I came to your store angry today, but you listened to what I had to say and took immediate action, Sonja. You saved your store a

customer, and I'll be sure to share my positive experience with others!"

"Knows how to lead and get things done."

"Doug is excellent at coming up with ways to streamline operations."

Most people keep these statements anonymous. Some, though, add the speaker's name or job title in italics or parentheses after the quote. It's your call. If you decide to use the person's name (which is a good idea if there's name-recognition value), be sure to get their permission before using it. If you'd like to add an endorsements section, but can't remember what others have said, make use of your network. Contact several people and simply ask them to provide a quote by asking them, "What would you say about me?"

We receive consistent feedback that these endorsements are among the most appreciated section of the resume. They work to support what you've already said and, maybe more importantly, they show a more personal side of you. Choose your endorsements carefully, though. We can almost guarantee that you'll be asked to talk about them in an interview.

Sending Your Resume

Once your resume is complete, you'll want to do several things to make sure it is as perfect as you can make it:

- Spell-check! And after you've spell-checked it, read it through again very carefully to catch any errors the spell-checker may have missed.

- Compare the resume to a description of the position you are going after. Make sure that you use words similar to the words used in that description. Also look to see whether there are other word-choice changes that would strengthen your resume. For example, say you've been working in insurance for the past eight years, but the position you are seeking is in healthcare or manufacturing. You are confident that your skills will transfer easily to the new work environment. You might, however, need to help your reader see you more clearly in that environment rather than in insurance. Go back through your resume and change words that are specific to the insurance industry, focusing more heavily on what you can accomplish than on where you have worked.

- Have a few other people read your resume and give you feedback, especially if you know people who hire people like you. Are they seeing what they would expect to see? Is there key information that seems to be missing? Is it easy for them to quickly read? Are there errors or awkward places that could lead to a more negative impression? You won't want to automatically change things they suggest (depending on the suggestion, of course), but if you have multiple people telling you the same thing, you might want to use their suggestions.

Most people have their own quality printers at home. A good printer only costs about $100. Use a paper with texture rather than plain printer paper. Remember that, when using hard copies, the paper is another small detail that communicates something about you.

When making copies, don't make too many at one time. The best resume is the one designed just for the position you're applying for. The next application calls for a new resume.

TIP: Stay away from dark paper colors, grays, or pastels, unless you're in a highly creative or artistic field. White and off-white work for just about any situation. Earth tones are good if you want to convey warmth. And there are some very good recycled papers.

When sending a hard copy, we suggest you mail your resume flat. Folding your resume can make it difficult to read. So you will want to get some 9 × 12 envelopes. Go with a white or colored envelope, rather than the standard manila envelope. The envelopes don't have to match your resume paper, but you want something that looks professional.

Building an Electronic Resume

You should prepare at least two versions of your resume: one for "hard copy" and one for electronic submissions. This second version may be necessary if you want to send your resume by e-mail or over the Internet either for the decision maker's convenience or to be included in his or her electronic resume tracking system.

Keywords

In building the traditional resume, we encouraged you to present yourself with action verbs: *managed, created, developed, evaluated,* and so on. An electronic resume sometimes needs to be different, and you may need to shift your focus from action verbs to keywords and nouns, using precise words and phrases such as *manager, creator, developer, evaluator,* or *machine operator.*

Computer systems use keywords to search databases for candidates whose resumes meet certain criteria. The key to an electronic JobGetting resume is to use as many valid keywords as possible in your resume. Use the language, buzzwords, or acronyms of your field or the field you want to move into. For example, your hard-copy resume might say

> Wrote and coordinated the production of promotional materials.

Your electronic or scannable resume would read

> Writer and production coordinator for 120-page, 4-color catalog and multimedia presentations.

We have also found it helpful to create a keyword list near the beginning of the resume. After your profile or summary of experience, create a section called Skill Areas or Areas of Expertise (similar to what we described previously). Under this section, simply list your keywords, like this:

Project coordinator	Engineering manager
Accounts payable	Budget management
Training facilitator	Microsoft Excel
Communication	Customer Service

Electronic Format

For a hard-copy resume, the visual presentation is important. You might boldface or italicize words, or use underlining or even reverse colors. This format also works fine when you send your resume via e-mail by attaching a Word file, for example (never simply copy and paste your resume directly into the body of an e-mail).

If you send your resume as an e-mail attachment, it's best to ask the employer something like, "Is a Word file okay, or would you prefer a text-only file?" Or you can convert your resume to PDF format to ensure that the formatting stays the same. Generally this is not a problem if you are submitting your resume through a company's Web site, where you can either copy and paste your resume into a designated area or upload your file.

An employer may sometimes ask for a scannable or text-only resume. A scannable resume is one that can be scanned into a database. To be scanned successfully, the format needs to be very simple, and you might make more use of nouns than verbs. It uses a text-only format, which is a resume made without any special formatting to it—for example, no bold, italics, or underlining. This is easy to create if you are using a Word program:

1. Open your regular resume file.

2. Click Save As.

3. Select Text Only.

You might also want to give this a new name so that you can quickly tell it apart from your original resume file.

If you're unsure about the recipient's software, follow these guidelines for your electronic resume:

- Avoid fancy text styles; stick with a commonly used font such as Helvetica, Times New Roman, or Arial.

- Use all capital letters for your section headings; do not use boldface, italics, or underlining.

- Avoid using special characters such as mathematical symbols or automatic bullets. If you want to use bullets, use a dash or asterisk from your keyboard. If you are creating a PDF file, however, such symbols are fine.

- Use the space bar instead of tabs or other format features to separate items.

- If you're sending the resume electronically as a text-only file, make sure your entire resume is left-aligned; do not center your name, address, or section headings. (Detail is more important in an electronic resume, so don't worry if this makes your resume more than two pages long.)

- If you're faxing a scannable resume, print the resume (laser print or high-quality Xerox) on white or very light-colored paper using the standard 8½ × 11 size. Make sure your fax machine is set to high resolution.

References

Sometimes an organization asks for your references with your resume. If this is the case, be sure to include them. Make sure, however, that your references are on a separate page, and not at the bottom of a resume page (see figure 5.3 for an example of a reference page). You'll want to include each person's title, organization, business address, telephone number, and e-mail address.

Identify three to five people for your reference page. Your list might include a superior, peers, a subordinate, a customer, and perhaps others in your field with some national or international recognition. In general, the higher the level of people on your reference list, the more credible they seem. If you will be conducting a national search, your reference list needs to be national in scope. Generally you do not list family members or friends who have never worked with you.

**Professional References for
Cindy Hernandez**

Betty K. Sharper
President and CEO
Metro Financial, Inc.
Washington, DC
(202) 123-4567
BKSharper@MFI.com

Bill W. Williams
Customer Service Representative
Premier Insurance Company
Arlington, VA
(703) 123-4567
Bill.Williams@Premier.com

Pam Lynn
Instructor
Massachusetts Business School
Boston, MA
(857) 123-4567
Instructor@MBS.edu

Sam Richards
Vice President, Operations
The Marketing Group
Syracuse, NY
(315) 123-4567
SamR@Marketing.com

Cindy L. Smeed
Owner, Serendipity
Washington, DC
(202) 123-4567
CindyLS33@gmail.com

Figure 5.3: Sample reference page.

Remember to always ask your references for permission to use their names. Discuss with them what they might say and what you would like them to focus on should they receive a call. Be sure to give each reference person a copy of your resume for reference.

Many people create a master reference list of 15 to 20 names. Then they cut and paste three to five of the most relevant and influential names onto their reference page based on the specific position they're going after.

Some Final Resume Dos and Don'ts

Whether you need a paper copy or an electronic resume, remember to follow these guidelines:

- Be flawless! Catch and fix all typos, punctuation problems, and grammar errors. Have someone who is attentive to details proofread your resume.

- Place the most relevant information first: You want the most interesting and relevant facts about yourself at the beginning of the resume.

- Avoid "I" or "me" in your resume (and avoid starting a sentence with "I" in your cover letter). Instead of complete sentences, use brief phrases that focus on your results and contributions.

- Quantify your experience whenever possible. Instead of "Increased sales," use "Increased sales by 60% in 5 months," or "Managed 25 accounts for annual revenues of $1.3M."

- Leave off salary and reference information. If you are specifically asked to provide this with your resume, do so in your cover letter.

- Avoid very personal information such as political or religious affiliation, marital status, age, number of children, and so on, and do *not* include a photo of yourself.

- Avoid fluff. Include only information that is most relevant to your career direction or the specific position you are seeking.

- Remember…sell yourself! Be professional and honest. Don't underemphasize your strengths, experience, and areas of contribution— but don't make yourself seem like someone you're not, either.

Your resume is never really finished. You can always keep refining it—adding a different piece of information, changing a word here, and so on. The result will be an attention-getting, results-focused word picture of you—what you've accomplished in the past, and a clear indication of the significant contributions you can make in the future.

CATHERINE'S STORY

When Catherine got laid off, she decided it was time to return to school and head her career in a new direction. Now that her course of study was completed, it was time to write a new resume. It had been 15 years since she had written one and she quickly noticed that resumes looked different now than when she graduated from college. Education didn't go first. A job objective wasn't even mentioned. Many resumes she saw were longer than one page. And the samples she looked at had lots of numbers and results of work.

Because she was making a career change, Catherine decided it would show herself off best if she used a combination functional and chronological resume. Her first page began with a paragraph called Career Summary. In seven sentences, Catherine summarized her strengths and included one sentence that began, "Frequently commended for...." The final sentence in her career summary read, "Enjoy coaching people to be high performers." That, she had decided, is what she really most enjoyed about her work: helping others be their best.

The next section was titled Major Strengths. Catherine listed three areas and under each major strength area were five statements. Each statement began with an action word. Because she was focusing on major strengths, she didn't need to list one-liners in any kind of chronological order. If it was a strength, and she had done it, she listed it. Catherine did, however, choose carefully the sequence of her one-liners. The one she wanted people to remember the most was listed first. And the second most important was listed second. The next most important thing she wanted people to remember about her was listed last under that strength. The others were in the middle. And she illustrated her results with numbers, percentages, and dollars.

Those two sections filled out the first page.

On page two, the next section was called Career History. Catherine began by listing her previous position first. Under her most recent position, a title she had held for five years, she listed several examples of duties and responsibilities as well as accomplishments—with results. She did rephrase statements she had used in the Career Summary and used them in the Career History section. After all, you have to validate where and when you made those accomplishments.

Catherine continued listing previous jobs and results of her work for each. Her main emphasis, however, was on the past 10 years. For her

(continued)

(continued)

entry-level job out of college, she listed only two examples of her work. "That was a long time ago," Catherine thought, "and what I did then has little to do with what I want to do in the future."

Her chronological career history took up most of the second page. Now she needed to make a decision: keep it at two pages or move to three. Listing her education completed the page. It was on to a third page.

Because Catherine had been active in professional and community activities, her next heading was just that: Professional and Community Activities. She had been a leader in her professional association, a Little League coach, and active in church.

Next came the section "What Others Say...." Catherine had been collecting statements from others for several months. She looked at her performance reviews and jotted down some things others had said about her over the years. She settled on five one-line statements. For each she could tell you who had said it, or something like it, or what performance review it was in.

She hit "Print" and waited. Then, with a soda in hand, she read through her resume. "Not bad," Catherine thought. "I have lots to contribute to my new employer!"

"It ain't braggin' if you've done it, and it ain't lyin' if you can prove it!"
—Mark Twain

How Do I Interview
Successfully?

The interview is a meeting to exchange information and to evaluate qualifications and interests—on both sides of the table. Interviews may be either brief or long; however, the basic decision of intent to hire (or to continue the conversation) is often made *within the first several minutes.*

This decision is often made on "feel" or being comfortable with the applicant—a "gut feeling." It's a matter of trust. The decision maker must have a sense of trust that you are who you say you are, and that you can do what you say you can do, before *intent* can turn to *reality.*

You can help turn intent to reality by going into each interview as well prepared as possible. Before the interview, you will want to know about the job, the company, the key people, and the company's vision or plans for the future. You find out these things by following the Deems JobGetting Skills™ system, presented in chapter 8.

How you look, how you act, and what you say make the difference between two qualified applicants, particularly in those first few minutes. If the decision maker doesn't feel comfortable with you, or doesn't have that sense of trust, you will not be invited to spend time exploring where and how you best fit within the company structure.

This chapter looks at some interviewing basics.

Typical Interview Procedures

Interview procedures vary according to the level of the position and differences in organizations. In general, the higher the level, the more complex and comprehensive the interviewing process. Although many workplaces have their own unique screening and interviewing processes, here are some common ones for different levels of positions.

Executive-Level Positions

Positions at this level include CEO, COO, CFO, and executive vice president. Interviewing often involves several people, both peers and supervisors. The interview session usually takes a full day or more, during which you meet with many people. Various kinds of testing are often used. As the interest continues, the meetings become more frequent and take more time. They are, from the beginning, not so much formal interviews as discussions between senior-level people on how to get things done. Visions are often shared, and the candidate's input as to how to make vision become reality is often requested. Extended trips are common as the key decision maker finally says "Yes, this is the person I need to fill this role." Spouses may or may not be included, depending on the company's culture.

Management Positions

Positions at this level include vice presidents and directors. The first meeting may or may not include the key decision maker. It will be more like an interview, with key questions being asked and the candidate's responses clearly noted in one way or another. If the candidate seems to be a fit, or one of several who may fit, the interviewing process continues. It might include an entire day (or several days) of interviews with those who would be key peers as well as superiors. The candidate might be asked to complete a number of assessments. Interviewers might include subordinates whose support is considered essential.

As the process continues, the meetings become less like an interview and more like a discussion among experienced people about how to get certain things done. Spouses may or may not be included. Extended trips to visit the city may be scheduled even prior to an offer.

Professional Positions

The interviewing process is typically more traditional at the beginning, and might start with a one-hour screening interview. The candidate will be asked more of the typical questions, such as those listed later in this chapter. The focus is usually on what the person has done before and how the person accomplished certain things. Ultimately the candidate will meet with the key decision maker, and might even meet with potential peers and other superiors. Depending on the company, the candidate might make trips to visit the site. The spouse is usually not involved, unless it is for a high-level professional position.

Hourly Workers

Typically, some kind of screening interview begins the process, often done over the telephone or by asking candidates to complete some written questions. From this, top candidates will be invited in for an interview. This might be with a person from human resources, or it might be the department manager. If the first meeting is with an HR person, chances are there will be a second interview with the actual manager or decision maker. You may or may not have a chance to meet the people you would be working with.

TIP: The more you know about the company and its needs, the more you will be able to talk about how you can help. And knowing who you will be meeting with for the interview may also give you clues as to the kinds of questions you'll be asked. That's all part of the hiring process.

How the Hiring Process Works

Part of being well prepared for your interview is to understand the hiring process in general. Figure 6.1 illustrates how the hiring process works for both the organization and the individual.

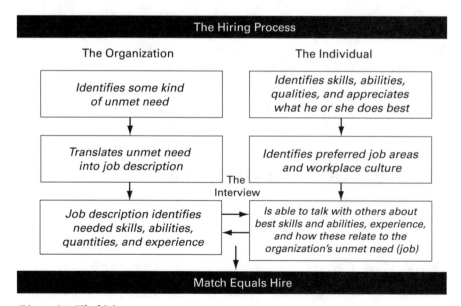

Figure 6.1: The hiring process.

First, the organization identifies an unmet need. The unmet need may be due to a vacancy or because a new challenge has emerged that needs to be addressed. Or maybe the company's vision calls for new people like you to make things happen.

The organization then develops some kind of a job description and the company attempts to find someone with the skills or competencies required to fill the position. The higher the level, the less is written about how the person will get things done. For the most senior-level positions, there may not be a well-defined job description. For an hourly position, there may be a great deal of detail in the job description.

On the other side, the individual identifies her or his best skills and experiences, and preferred job areas and work environment. These qualifications and preferences provide the basis for the interview discussion, particularly as they relate to the organization's unmet needs.

Sometimes the JobGetter can influence the company's decision on filling the job by helping to clarify unmet needs. "What are the three biggest challenges that I will be facing during the next six months?" is a question that can help you and the company identify or clarify unmet needs. You can be ready to discuss ways to resolve each of those problems.

The decision makers will want to see, as clearly as possible, which of the candidates have the right fit to get done the things that need to get done. When there is a perceived match between a person's skills and experiences and the company's needs, there is a hire.

It is your responsibility to show, as clearly as you can, how your skills, experiences, and abilities match the company's needs. Fortunately, if you follow the guidelines in this book, you will be ready to do just that.

Making the Best Impression

How you look, how you act, and what you say are the basics of making a good impression. The following sections discuss these three most important aspects of your interview impression.

How You Look

Your appearance normally is known as a "negative" factor. A good appearance will not by itself get you a job. But a bad appearance may be a major reason you do not receive further consideration. Do your research about the right interview attire for the situation and the company. Many factors play into this, for example:

- The East and upper Midwest are more typically conservative than the Southwest.

- The legal and financial industries most often require white shirts and conservative suits for both men and women.

- Fields considered more creative (advertising and entertainment, for example) have a less formal dress standard, as do companies that work primarily with self-directed teams.

- International companies have their own concepts of what is and is not acceptable attire. What works in one country may not be acceptable in another.

How do you find out what's appropriate for a particular company? You can learn a lot by observing the employees as they enter or leave the offices, by talking with one or more current employees, or even by checking with people within your own network. Do men wear beards? Are jackets and slacks common? How long do the women wear their skirts? If possible, observe particularly those people in jobs similar to the one you are seeking. After researching the company's employees, make your look just a bit more formal than the employees you have observed—dress just a notch above.

Basic Rules for Men

In most cases, the proper color to wear is dark blue or gray. A black suit with narrow stripes of red or blue is also acceptable. Generally, a white or other light-colored shirt is best, with a conservative tie. If a suit does not seem appropriate, casual slacks and a sports coat will do well. Avoid brown or green—these are "soft" colors. Fancy jewelry and expensive watches are not proper in most interviews. Make sure your fingernails are clean and your shoes are polished. Use aftershave conservatively—you don't want the scent to announce you.

Basic Rules for Women

Women have more colors from which to choose. In addition to the blue and gray, tan, wine, and blue-green are good colors. A suit with a neutral-colored blouse is appropriate. Generally, buy the more expensive blouse and a less expensive suit. The blouse should not reveal too much nor cover up too much with frills. Avoid a men's-cut suit and tie (it's okay to look feminine). Casual slacks and a jacket or sweater also may work well, if a suit seems like too much. Avoid colored nail polish, unless you are applying for a position in which a certain fashion statement is needed. Also avoid large or dangling jewelry that may be visually distracting or noisy. Do not use perfume.

Classic or conventional business attire is always appropriate. When in doubt, opt for the more conservative dress.

How You Act

By your actions, you convey confidence, self-assurance, energy, and the ability to work well with others. As with your appearance, your actions are much more likely to keep you from further consideration rather than to ensure receiving the job offer. Make sure that your actions show off your qualifications in the best possible way.

It may feel silly, but practice walking and sitting in front of a mirror if you are in any doubt about how you look. You want to look natural, not stiff, and practicing your natural look will give you more confidence. Remember not to slouch or fidget.

What to do with your hands during an interview is often a problem. As a general rule, be natural. You should not fold your hands stiffly in front of you or wring them. To give your hands something to do, take a pad and pencil with you to the interview and keep them in front of you. They will also be useful for jotting down notes to yourself before the interview, and for taking other appropriate notes during the meeting. If you talk with your hands, as many of us do, it's okay to do so in the interview.

TIP: If you're being interviewed by several people at the same time, write their names on your notepad according to how they are seated. That way, if you forget a name you can easily look at your notes and tell by your "diagram" what that person's name is.

Other things to keep in mind:

- Offer a firm (not fishy!) handshake upon arriving and leaving. If you tend to have sweaty hands, run them under cool water just before the interview. If you tend to have cold hands, warm them up before going into the interview.

- Make eye contact and have a friendly smile when greeted by your interviewer. Use the person's name as you greet her or him.

- Maintain good eye contact during the interview. Keep in mind, however, that eye contact is a cultural behavior, and what's appropriate in one company may be quite different in another.

- Before you enter the interview, turn off your cell phone to avoid interruptions.

- Don't chew gum, suck on candy, or smell like smoke.

What You Say

The key to any successful interview is

Preparation!

Preparation!

Preparation!

How you look and how you act can help, but what you say and how you say it make the most significant difference between getting the job offer and coming in second.

Here are some key points to keep in mind:

- Before going into the interview, learn as much as you can about the company and the position. Get online and research the company's background, key people, and goals. Talk to people about what they know of the company, visit the company Web site, or call or write for information (more on this in chapter 8).

- Anticipate the kinds of questions that might be asked, and prepare your responses before the interview. Keep in mind that screening interviews often involve questions concerning your basic qualifications for the position as well as some broader, more general questions. An interview with a decision maker, however, is likely to be very specific in terms of what you have done and are likely to do. Use words that have the most impact. Make sure your responses sound natural, not canned.

- Have some key examples ready to illustrate your main points. If you say you are good at leading teams, be ready with examples of team projects that you led that were very successful.

- Have some key answers that contain the specific information about yourself that you want to get across during the interview. Use the answers at the appropriate time, even though you might not be asked the exact question. Remember—*you* are responsible for identifying how your skills and experiences match the organization's unmet needs.

- Make your answers brief but complete. Don't ramble. Listen carefully to what is being asked, and then respond directly to the question. Watch for cues from the interviewer to tell you when you've said too much or when they might want more information. Don't hesitate to say, "Would you like me to tell you more about that?"

- You need to go into each and every interview having spent several hours thinking about how you achieved your results and organizing your answers. Provide enough information without boring them with unnecessary details.

- Using three examples to illustrate a point is effective. Listeners will find it easier to remember something if you say, "First.... Second.... Third...."

- Think of the three main things you most want them to remember about you. Be sure you get across those key items during the interview or discussion. These key points can be your summary at the close of the meeting.

- Finally, never, ever lie about your qualifications and experiences!

Some Basic (but Problematic) Interview Questions

No one can predict all the questions you'll be asked in an interview. There are, however, several basic questions you can expect at some point in the process. The following questions and responses will help you get started. When considering your own responses, use the one-two-three approach mentioned in the preceding section.

Tell Me About Yourself

This is a good opener, and many decision makers will start with this kind of a comment. It's the same as saying, "Tell me how you got to this point..." or "What do I need to know about you?" Decision makers seldom want a historical account of your personal life. And don't simply walk through your resume—chances are they've seen it already. What they do want is some good information about you—and it's a great way to set the tone for the interview. Structure your response in terms of three things you want the person to know about you. You can say something like this:

Well, first I'm a person who has been in production management in one way or another all of my career. In fact, I started out at a local marketing firm, organizing neighborhood kids to deliver flyers and brochures to area homes during the summer. I enjoy production management and others tell me I do it very well. Second, I'm a person who....

Think of three things you want the decision maker to know about you, make the statement, and give a very brief example.

What Are Your Greatest Strengths?

It is important that you become completely comfortable talking about things you do well. You may need to practice this with someone prior to any real interview. Using the one-two-three approach, a good response might be this:

> *First, people say that I am extremely well organized and I'm frequently complimented on being able to handle several tasks at once. Let me give you an example.... Second.... Third....*

Remember that your resume will contain what you consider to be your major strengths. Your response to this kind of question must reflect what's on your resume without repeating it word for word.

What Is Your Greatest Weakness?

Do not admit to having a greatest weakness. A response such as this is most appropriate:

> *Well, I suppose that I have some weaknesses, but can't think of any that would keep me from doing the type of job that you are looking for help with.*

One other option is to state a "weakness" that also has an obvious positive side. As with any negative question such as this, begin your response with a positive statement about yourself.

> *Others have said that sometimes I commit too much. It hasn't been a problem because in the past few years I've learned to prioritize and get at those things that are the most crucial. And I've learned to ask my boss what she wants completed first.*

Variations of this question include "What is one area that you would most like to improve during this next year?" or "Tell me about something you have been trying to learn recently."

Why Are You Available Now?

If you were caught in a reorganization or downsizing, say so. Something like this is all that is necessary:

> *ABC Corporation reorganized and my job was one of several that were eliminated.*

With all the publicity about layoffs and early retirement programs, your situation is well understood and no lengthy discussion is called for.

If you were terminated for job performance but allowed to resign, say something like this:

> *I was with XYZ Corporation for several years and had progressed as far as possible. After much discussion, my manager and I agreed that a change would be in my best interest.*

It is important when answering this or similar questions that you do not badmouth your past company or individuals within the company. They may have been jerks, but it makes you look bad if you call attention to that fact. Always speak positively of your previous employer and colleagues.

What Are You Making in Your Current Job? or What Are Your Salary Goals?

Salary is very often an eliminator—asking for a salary that is too low eliminates you from consideration just as fast as asking for one that is too high. You don't want to talk about salary until both you and the interviewer know that you are the one for the job. And *never* bring this up before they do.

A few examples of good responses are the following:

> *My research indicates that this kind of position in this city would have a salary range between x dollars and y dollars, and I believe I fit within that range.*

> *When we talk about a specific offer, we can discuss compensation in greater detail.*

> *I'll be glad to consider your best offer.*

If pressed, provide your salary goal in terms of a range rather than a specific figure:

> *The kind of position I'm looking for will have responsibilities that put me in a range of x to y.*

Sometimes you might want to say something like this:

> *Salary will not be the only factor in my decision to accept this position, and I'm sure that as our discussions progress, we will have time to talk about salary.*

If the interviewer pushes you to name a salary, our advice is to be careful. Give a range or talk in terms of total compensation. They may be pushing you to see how cheaply they can get you. And if salary is their main consideration, do you really want to work there?

Every person is unique when it comes to dollars. Know what you need, and at the proper time communicate that in a general way to the interviewer. Just remember to let them be the one to first raise the question of compensation and benefits.

Tell Me How You Handled...

The emphasis on interviewing today is performance, situational, or behavioral interviewing. In this type of interview, the focus is on what a person did or how a person handled specific situations in the past. Because the best single indicator of future performance is a candidate's past performance, you may get a number of questions phrased like this: "Tell me what you did in order to...."

You can anticipate the kinds of performance questions you might be asked simply by thinking about what's logically important in the position for which you are interviewing. Be ready with good examples and think through how you actually got certain things accomplished. For example, if you are asked something like "Tell me how you decided to expand your market..." you can be ready to answer with something like "Well, first.... Second.... Third...." Or if you are asked, "How do you handle an angry customer?" you can be ready with "That does sometimes happen, and in the past I have...." Keep your answers to the point, but still provide enough information so that the decision maker understands how you get things done.

Why Should I Hire You?

Be ready for this question, which is possibly the most important question you'll be asked. And be quick with your answer. It must be strong, confident, and to the point. Think carefully about what separates you from the other (also-qualified) candidates they are speaking with.

> *Why should you hire me? First, I have the skills and experience you need to get the job done. Second, I have the vision you're looking for and the energy and enthusiasm to bring it into reality. Third, XYZ Company is the kind of place, and has the kind of people, where I would like to contribute, and I want the job.*

Your answer should be quick (indicating that you've already thought about this) and spoken with energy and good eye contact. It doesn't need to be long—just a few sentences is long enough. Then stop! Wait for the interviewer to tell you what's next. Be sure you highlight your major strengths and tie them into what the company is seeking, using words that the decision maker will understand.

This question can be phrased in different ways. A similar question is, "In what ways can you make a contribution to our organization?" The interviewer still wants to know why hiring you is a smart decision.

Some Additional Questions

There are several other standard questions you might be asked during an interview or first discussion. You may be asked these questions or slightly different versions of them. Remember, the best way to ensure that you will answer them well is to take time before the interview to prepare!

Tell Me What You Like Best About Your Present (Most Recent) Position

Briefly describe your responsibilities, main tasks, and several of your recent projects. Make sure you convey energy or passion in your answer. The question is intended to draw out whether you will enjoy and be enthusiastic about duties that are important in the new job.

What Are Your Major Accomplishments in Your Present Job?

Be ready. Before any interview, look again at the results of your work (accomplishments) identified in chapter 3. Sift through your many accomplishments and identify the three that most clearly relate to the job under consideration.

> *First, I led the reorganization team that reengineered our division. Second, I.... And third, I....*

If I Call Your Previous Supervisor and Ask Him/Her About Your Strengths, What Will I Be Told?

Focus on your strengths listed in your resume. If you are unsure what that supervisor would say, respond by stating, "Well, I hope my supervisor would say..." and list the three strengths you want the interviewer to remember.

> *I hope my supervisor would say that first, I was always ready to step in and fix whatever was broken. Second, I knew how to lead teams and did it very well. And third, I could effectively deal with unhappy customers by listening carefully to their concerns and taking positive action to help resolve those concerns.*

Where Do You Hope to Be in Five Years? Ten Years?

The interviewer wants to know if you have professional and personal goals. With all the change taking place in the job market these days, sometimes this is a good answer:

> *There are so many changes taking place in today's marketplace that it's hard to say exactly where I might be. I do know that I want to be in a position where I have responsibility for....*

Typically, your answer should include a desire to learn more, have the opportunity to meet new challenges, and have the chance to increase your responsibilities as you continue developing your skills. And be ready for a common follow-up: "How do you plan to achieve your goals?"

When asked about your career goals and plans, you can mention a job title you'd ultimately like to have. This can help show ambition on your part. However, a specific title is not needed. Instead, you can tell them something like this:

> *What I do know is that I'm looking for a place where I can develop my strengths to be in a position of leadership that contributes to the organization's bottom line, and where I can make a positive impact on employees.*

Which of the Jobs on Your Resume Did You Like Best, and Why?

Tell them—focus on challenges, opportunities, and tasks. If what you liked best doesn't mesh with the company's needs, both you and they are wasting time.

Also, be ready to be asked the opposite: "What did you like least?" Remember to address the negative question from a positive perspective. If you disliked the tediousness of the work, you could respond with, "I'm most effective in a fast-paced environment where each day presents new challenges. It was frustrating to be in a position that did not demand that I use my skills to their fullest."

Be careful with the negative version of this question; under no circumstances should you speak negatively about an organization, a boss, or a co-worker!

How Would You Describe Your Management Style?

Briefly describe your management style, with examples. If you're interviewing for a management position, count on this one being asked. Be ready for it, and have your examples ready. A good phrase to throw in is something that begins with "My subordinates tell me..." or "My direct reports have said that I...."

How Long Would It Take for You to Become Productive in This Job?

They want to know if you're ready to get at it and ready to invest the extra energy at first to get up to speed. Let them know you would be productive immediately (even if there might be an initial learning curve).

What New Projects Have You Been Involved in Lately? *Or* What New Things Have You Learned?

In other words, are you keeping up with the changes in your field? Be ready to talk about your new projects, new learnings, or the latest trends and developments in your industry. Mention the industry periodicals you read regularly and something interesting you read in them recently.

Of Your Accomplishments This Past Year, of Which Are You Most Proud?

Again, this gets at what you enjoy doing, which, hopefully, is very similar to what they need to get done. Be ready to tell them what it was and your role in reaching that accomplishment.

Why Do You Want to Work for This Company?

Be ready for this one! Give an answer that shows enthusiasm as well as an understanding of the company and what it does:

> First, your company has an excellent reputation for producing outstanding products. Second, I believe that your company is a great place to work and that I would fit in and enjoy working here. And third, you need someone who can do the things I do best and most enjoy doing.

Job-Specific Questions

You will also be asked questions that relate to specific tasks of the position. Think through what those questions might be and be ready with answers that showcase your knowledge and related experience.

NOTE: *Never, ever lie about your qualifications and experience!* It is proper to answer questions in a way that puts yourself in the best possible light. It is proper to not volunteer information if it might be considered damaging to you. It even is proper to avoid a specific area by providing an answer that does not exactly fit the question—*if* the interviewer lets you get away with it. But *never* lie about your qualifications and experiences.

Still More Questions

Here are a few other questions you should be prepared to answer:

- How do you want to be managed?

- What motivates you to put forth your greatest effort?

- How do you determine or evaluate success?

- What qualities should a successful manager possess?

- What interests you about our product or service?

- What two or three things are most important to you in your job?

- What criteria are you using to evaluate the organization for which you hope to work?

- In what kind of work environment are you most comfortable?

- What do you know about our company?

- What suggestions do you have for our company?

- Was there anything today that you were afraid I was going to ask you?

Behavioral Interview Questions

Behavioral interview questions deserve some special attention here. Many traditional interview questions focus on what you think and how you would handle certain kinds of situations. Behavioral questions focus on examples of your past behavior, as a way to predict your future actions. These questions help the interviewer rate a candidate's skills based on past performance rather than gut feelings.

The behavioral interview uses structured, open-ended questions about real-life situations to see which skills candidates have used successfully in the past. Often it feels less like an interview and more like a structured conversation or discussion.

Avoid giving general answers. Instead, describe a particular event, project, or experience in terms of

1. The situation or task

2. Your actions

3. The results or outcome

To prepare for behavioral questions, think about specific experiences you have had and how they relate to the available opening. Prepare short descriptions and stories about your past work experience, leadership, teamwork, initiative, planning, and customer service. Other common areas to explore with behavioral questions include employee relations, key successes and failures and what you learned, how your work philosophies show in the workplace, and creative or innovative problem-solving.

Sample Behavioral Questions

There's a simple formula for behavioral questions. They begin with something like, "Tell me about a time when you..." and end with "and tell me how you handled it." That's what they want to know—not how you *think* you might handle a specific situation, but how you *actually* handled the situation. Don't hesitate to add what you learned from the specific experience. Decision makers like people who learn how to do things better.

- Tell me about a time when you had to make a difficult decision but didn't have all the information you needed.

- What is the most significant contribution you made to your past/present company? Tell me how you got it done.

- What is the biggest mistake you've made, and how did you handle it?

- Describe the biggest challenge in your last position and how you handled it.

- Give me an example of a time you had to persuade someone to accept your idea, and tell me how you did it.

- Tell me about one of your best days at work. What made that day so good?

- Describe a time when you were faced with an unexpected problem and how you handled it.

- Tell me about a time when you put a great deal of time and effort into a project and did not succeed.

- Describe a time when you were faced with significant stress at work, the kind that really tested your coping skills. And how did you deal with it?

- Give me an example of when you had to show strong leadership and what you did.

- What's the most important thing you learned in your last supervisor assignment, and how did you learn it?

- Tell me about a time when you had to adapt to a very diverse group of people.

- Tell me about a time you had to be persistent in order to reach your goals.

- Give me an example of a time when you used your management philosophy to deal with a difficult problem with an employee.

- When have you found it useful to use detailed checklists and procedures to reduce error potential on the job?

- Describe a time when you were a part of a team and one of the members wasn't carrying his or her weight, and tell me how you handled it.

- What have you done to make your job more fulfilling and satisfying?

TIP: During behavioral interviews, it's common for the interviewer to ask "negative" questions—questions that involve mistakes, project failure, or something that didn't work out as planned. It's fine to talk about mistakes; we all make them. In your answer, keep the focus on what you learned and how you might handle it differently based on what you learned.

On any answer that you give, expect the interviewer to question and probe. You may be asked follow-up questions such as these:

- "What were you feeling?"

- "What were you thinking?"

- "How did the other person respond?"

- "If you could do it over again, would you handle this situation in the same way? Why or why not?"

How to Answer Behavioral Questions

Remember not to describe how you *would* behave, but how you *did* behave. If you have decided that you should have behaved differently, explain this—it will show that you have learned something from the experience.

The one-two-three kind of response described earlier in this chapter can work well in a behavioral interview. When asked a behavioral question, you can respond by saying, "Well, first I did..., and second I..., and third I did...." Then expand on each of your responses, telling in more detail what you did. Highlight the results.

Remember, you do not have to limit your stories to specific work situations. An experience at home, at school, or within the community may also relate to the question if you don't have a specific work example.

TIP: You will no doubt find yourself in a variety of different interview situations, such as telephone interviews, team interviews, interviews with subordinates, and others. No matter which type of interview it is, remember to anticipate questions and prepare your responses.

Questions You Can Ask the Interviewer

Keep in mind that the interview is a two-way street. Not only does the organization want to know whether you're right for them, you want to know whether they're right for you. So ask questions. Imagine they will offer you the position and now you need to know more about them in order to know whether to accept or decline the position.

If you follow the Deems JobGetting Skills™ outlined in chapter 8, many of your questions will have been answered prior to the formal interview. It's good, in any case, to have questions of your own that indicate your enthusiasm and interest in the position. The interviewer will probably end by asking whether you have any questions. If you don't, you look like you're not very interested or engaged.

Whenever possible, frame your questions as if you were already filling the position. Instead of asking, "What are the goals for this position?" you can ask, "What are the main tasks or goals you want me to accomplish in the first six months to a year?"

Questions you might ask include the following:

- Why is the position open?

- Who are the people I would be working with?

- What are the main tasks or goals you would want me to accomplish in the first six months to a year?

- What are some of the barriers to getting those things accomplished?

- How would you describe this company's culture? Goals? Values? Management style? How does this culture (or goals, and so on) show in a day-to-day way?

- Where do you see this position leading to in the next five years?

- How will my performance be measured or evaluated? Who would I report to?

- What would a typical day look like for me in this company?

- How would you describe an ideal employee?

- What do you see as the key skills and abilities necessary for someone to be successful in this job?

- What is your company's policy on career development/providing learning opportunities/transfers to other cities?

Do not ask questions that are already answered on the company's Web site or in any of the literature provided to you ahead of time. Avoid questions that can be answered with a yes or no. Also, never ask about salary and benefits issues until the interviewer approaches those subjects. Generally employers prefer to talk about salary and benefits only after an offer has been made.

When the Interview Is Over

At the end of the interview, thank the interviewer for the opportunity to meet and exchange information. Ask whether there is anything more that you can provide to help with the decision, and find out what the next step is—what is the timeframe for making their decision?

Then, if you want the position, tell the interviewer before you walk out the door! Be direct:

> *I appreciate the time we've spent talking about the job. The more I learn about your company and the things you need to get done here, the more enthused I become. I want the position.*

Decision makers have feelings like everyone else. They don't like to hear "No." Decision makers report to us that if there are two closely matched candidates, they'll more often offer the position to the person who says "I want the job." Why? Because they are pretty sure that person will accept, and the task of hiring will be over.

When you get home, write a short thank-you letter. This is a friendly business letter (typed). It doesn't need to be long but it does need to show that you practice good, basic human relations skills and that you know how to say please and thank you.

The thank-you letter also can play a strategic role. It gives you a chance to once more show how your strengths match the employer's needs. It gives you a chance to say things you wish you'd said in the interview, but didn't think of in time. And it gives you a chance to talk briefly about some point you thought over on the way home from the interview, and reaffirm your interest in the position.

Figure 6.2 is a sample thank-you letter.

John Hand
3622 Willow Way
Grand Haven, Michigan 49417
(269) 555-5555
jhand37@email.com

John LaRue
ABC Company
2910 Century Blvd.
Pocatello, ID 83204

Dear Mr. LaRue,

Thank you for this morning's discussion about ABC Company's IT leadership needs. The vision and goals for your IT department sound both exciting and challenging, and I enjoyed having the opportunity to tour the new facility and meet other members of the team.

While driving back to my office, I was thinking about what you said concerning market research. This is similar in many ways to the decisions I faced at DEF Corp. There, after analyzing the data, my team designed and implemented a plan to test new products in a wider variety of settings in more cities. The results were more information, better information, and increased market share.

I also realized that we never got back to our early discussion of recruiting new team members. It seems to me that a new system of matching applicants' natural strengths with job needs is in order, and I have several ideas as to how we could get this done.

The physical changes you have made within your facility are very impressive and speak highly of the commitment ABC Company has to creating a high-performance environment. With my strengths in aligning human and technological goals, I am confident in my ability to fill the "missing link" role of which you spoke.

Again, thank you! This morning has confirmed my interest in joining the ABC Company, and I'm ready to talk further with the members of your selection committee.

Sincerely,

John Hand

Figure 6.2: Sample thank-you letter.

Follow up with the interviewer based on what you were told at the conclusion of the interview. Sometimes the decision-making goes much slower than expected. If you encounter this, be persistent and maintain contact. If you were told you would hear back within a week and it has been 10 days, go ahead and call. Tell them you're very interested and wanted to know if they needed anything more from you to help them finalize their decision. Many of the people with whom we work report that after receiving the offer the decision maker said something like, "Your persistence really got my attention."

What you do *not* want to do is precisely what most other candidates will do: hurry up and wait, hoping for a phone call. Make it happen!

Ace the Interview!

Before each interview, review the following information. It will help you prepare, interview with confidence, and ace the interview.

- If given the choice, select a time for the interview that fits your schedule and normal energy level. Generally, if you're the first to be interviewed, all others who follow have to live up to your standard. If you're the last, it's easy to compare you with all the others. If you can arrange it, try to be either the first or the last person interviewed.

- The more you know about the company, the greater chance you have to effectively market yourself—as well as decide whether this is where you want to invest part of your life.

- Be sure you know who you will be interviewing with—their name and their job title and how they relate to the position. This will help you anticipate questions.

- You also want to know as much as you can about the position: its duties, responsibilities, reporting procedures, work climate, and so on. The more you know about the position, the easier it is to prepare for the interview.

- Anticipate and prepare! Think about the specific kinds of questions you might be asked based on the position and who you will be meeting with, and then prepare your responses. Try them out on someone else to get their feedback.

- There is no substitute for promptness, courtesy, preparation, enthusiasm, and a positive attitude! Show energy and interest throughout all your actions. Use good grammar and good diction.

- Arrive for the interview 10 to 15 minutes early. Before entering the building, give yourself time to focus, take a few deep breaths, and allow yourself to relax. Review your notes. Stay centered on what you want to accomplish during the interview.

- Start the interview on a positive note—use a firm handshake, a sincere smile, and a friendly greeting. Keep in mind that the interviewer may also be nervous; do what you can to help increase his or her comfort.

- Think before you speak. There is nothing wrong with a pause in the conversation. If you are uncomfortable, you can say something like, "Wow, that's a great question. Let me think about that for a moment." Collect your thoughts; then begin.

- Never speak negatively of a former employer, co-worker, teacher, or institution. Even if you had problems with prior experiences, try to frame your answers positively.

- Avoid debate. This does not mean, however, that you must agree with everything the interviewer says. If you disagree with something, a simple statement like "That's interesting. My experience has been that…" will do. Some interviewing strategies include using negative questions or outrageous remarks, simply to see whether they can rattle you or draw you into a negative discussion. Refuse to be drawn in.

- If you want the position, tell the interviewer *before* you leave. Then, when you get home, write a thank-you letter indicating your appreciation for the interview and confirming your interest.

- Your interview goes beyond the interview meeting. Be professional and courteous to others you may meet, including the receptionist. If lunch or dinner is included, be assured that they are still evaluating you.

- If you know they will be interviewing others after you, arrange to contact them about the time they will be meeting their final candidate. You can ask, "When will you be finished with interviewing candidates?" Most decision makers will tell you. Because you want your name to rise to the top of the list again, think of a way to reconnect. One way is to find a relevant article that touches on one of the interview topics. Send it to the interviewer with a brief note, to arrive about the time of the last interview.

- Follow through on whatever the decision maker asks or suggests. If the day comes and goes on which you were to receive a call, take the initiative and call the decision maker. Simply inquire as to where they are in the selection process. Close the conversation by restating your interest in the company and the position.

For additional information, there are a number of good resources on interviewing. These include *Interview Magic* by Susan Britton Whitcomb and *Next-Day Job Interview* by Mike Farr and Dick Gaither. You are on your way to an enjoyable, successful interview!

Here are two worksheets to help you keep the information you need so you can easily make use of it. The Interview Log helps you think through what you know about the company and position, how your skills and experiences match their needs, questions you will want to ask, and a reminder to send your thank-you note. Start an interview log once the interview date is set and record your notes to jump-start your preparation.

INTERVIEW LOG

Company _____

Interview time/date _____

Position _____

Interviewer _____ Title _____

Notes about the company/position:

_____

_____

_____

_____

_____

_____

Experience and skill needs for this position:

_____

_____

_____

_____

_____

_____

_____

_____

_____

(continued)

(continued)

_____

_____

Key experience, skills I will communicate:

_____

_____

_____

Examples I could use:

_____

_____

_____

_____

_____

_____

My questions:

_____

_____

_____

_____

_____

_____

_____

_____

_____

_____

_____

Thank-you letter sent: _____

Other follow-up: _____

The My Interview Strategy worksheet asks you to identify the questions you think you will be asked, along with your responses. Others tell us that writing out your answers before the interview helps you respond with more confidence and clarity.

MY INTERVIEW STRATEGY

Questions I Might Be Asked	Ways I Could Respond

(continued)

(continued)

MARK'S STORY

Mark was manager of an R&D unit that was trying to move from fast-follower to first-to-market. But he and the company's executive vice president didn't get along, and one day Mark was told his job was over.

It had been 10 years since Mark had formally interviewed for a job, and he wasn't looking forward to it. He had read several articles on interviewing and talked with other managers about the questions they often asked candidates. He took time to write down the kinds of questions he often asked.

Then he realized he didn't interview at the level at which he wanted to be hired.

Mark went through several interviews, basically for the experience of being interviewed. "My palms were really sweaty," he reported after his first real interview, "and I realized I need to take a more proactive approach to the process."

Then he called, excited and challenged. The job he really wanted had opened and he was one of three to be considered. Mark had talked

CHAPTER 6: HOW DO I INTERVIEW SUCCESSFULLY?

twice with the key decision maker, the person he would be reporting to. He knew what the job involved and what some of the problems were. "I googled the key decision makers and read the company's annual report. I also visited the company's Web site and looked at the press releases section," Mark continued.

"I knew what they needed and what they wanted. And I could do it," he said.

Mark put together his leather binder with resume and job description on one side and a blank page on the other. Then he added several things to the page. He knew they would ask about his strengths, so he wrote down keywords that would remind him of the three key strengths he wanted to emphasize. Under each he added several descriptive words of past projects where he had used these skills.

On another section of the page he wrote down the questions he wanted to ask.

"It went very well," Mark reported afterward, "and the three top execs in the department were there. What really caught their attention was when they asked me if I had any questions. I did what you suggested and asked, 'What is it you want me to get accomplished in the first six months and first year in the position' and it blew them away," Mark added. After discussing what the leaders were wanting, he asked a second question: "What are the barriers I might face and are the resources available for meeting those objectives?"

As he shook hands with the three leaders, he added, "I want the job and I can accomplish what you need to get accomplished."

Mark reports his new position in the new organization is going very well and he has received several promotions.

"Nobody ever listened himself out of a job."
—Calvin Coolidge

CHAPTER 7

How Do I Find and Respond to Job Openings?

It's time to start creating your personal Plan for Action for finding your next position. Finding those job openings and responding takes time, energy, and commitment. This chapter introduces the four major ways to find job openings. It also discusses how you can respond to each opening of interest. You'll want to start, though, by making sure you are ready for the large amounts of information you'll be gathering throughout the JobGetting process.

Get Organized!

Your personal Plan for Action, which you will complete in chapter 8, will include several different strategies for finding job openings. That means you will be dealing with *lots* of information: names, phone numbers, e-mail addresses, dates, positions you've applied for, follow-up notes and schedules, notes from networking meetings, who introduced you to whom, and so on.

Before you get started, it's important to establish some kind of system for recording all the information you will gather, so that you can find it when you need it. Otherwise, your head will be swimming with data rather than thinking clearly about how your skills and experience can meet a specific set of job needs.

It's easiest to create your system at the beginning, rather than waiting until you've already begun responding to openings. If you have a computer with a database or spreadsheet program and you are comfortable using it, that will work fine. A table created in a Word document can also work, although it's somewhat more limiting.

You'll want to create at least one, and possibly two, JobGetting files:

- One to help you track openings and opportunities and how and when you responded.

- A second that you devote strictly to networking: who you've spoken with, contact information, notes from meetings, connections between people, and so on.

There are different ways to set up your files, and you'll want to create one that works best for you. Just be sure your system allows you to capture all the information you will need. Your JobGetting file might look something like figure 7.1.

Date	Company	Position/ Description	Contact Name	Phone	E-mail	Action Taken	Follow-up	Interview	Thank-You Sent
3/11/2009	InfraCorp	OD and learning consultant: liaison between departments, assess needs, assist in developing programs to address needs and evaluate program outcomes	Sue Smith, VP of Learning & Development	555-565-5555	smiths@icorp.com	Phoned and briefly discussed position.	Resume sent to Sue and to HR.	3/20/09: Went very well; concerns include entry into new markets and increasing workforce diversity.	3/20/2009
3/19/2009	Maximar	Instructional designer: develop curriculum for new programs including storyboards; work with SMEs; coordinate with tech people.	Emira Broddick	555-566-6666	emirab@mmr.com	Ad said no phone calls; e-mailed with questions on scope of the work.	Send resume Weds. via Web site.	To be scheduled	
3/25/2009	Noodles, Inc.	Training specialist: design, develop, and facilitate learning interventions; no CBT; emphasis on diversity and soft skills.	Blake Johnston	555-567-7777		Spoke with Blake's assistant 3/24; resume and cover letter sent 3/25.	3/30 placed call to Blake, left msg.		

Figure 7.1: Sample JobGetting file.

This reflects some of the most basic information you will want to save for yourself. As you use the system, you may find other bits of information you will want to include as well.

You will also want to create a separate file just for your networking contacts, and what resulted from each networking meeting or conversation. This is important information to keep track of, and you can create something as simple as the file shown in figure 7.2.

Name and Organization	Reason for Contact	Phone Number	E-mail Address	Notes	Next Follow-up
Stan Rizzo	Former classmate; may have contacts in healthcare	222-221-2222	stantheman@mmm.com	Met for coffee 4/15/09; reviewed resume--he liked it; brainstormed ideas for appropriate kinds of roles in healthcare, area hospitals, clinics.	5/12/2009
Cathy Goldbar	Met at Feb. ASTD mtg; knows some people at Noodles.	222-222-2323	cgoldbar@msn.com	Meet 4/1 at Fredericks-- remember to ask her about other ASTD contacts.	
Robin Lindsey	See how her JobGetting is going; exchange info on leads.	222-223-2424	Robin_Lindsey@stellar.com	R's a bit down this week, so was good to stop thinking about myself a bit and help her stay energized; gave me Tom Stetson's name and e-mail; passed along Newton info to her since she might be interested in that spot.	Set up coffee time for 4/17.

Figure 7.2: Sample networking file.

If you don't have access to a computer system or aren't comfortable using one for this purpose, we suggest using 5 × 8 index cards or setting up some other database system that works for you. Using 5 × 8 cards has the added advantage of being extremely portable, so you can easily carry them around with you. They are large enough to hold a good deal of information; they can be shuffled about; they have some stability and will withstand being carried and shuffled; and they don't take up a lot of space. If you're using a card system, just be sure to use the 5 × 8 size because 3 × 5 cards are generally too small for the information you'll want to record.

Whichever organizing system you use—index cards, an Excel program, or notebook—stay disciplined to using it daily. This record will help guide your actions, assist in your weekly evaluation, and provide valuable contact information quickly when you need it. Every time you follow up on an opening or opportunity, record the necessary information and plan what new action to take, and when, and what happened as a result. After each call, meeting, or interview, record the necessary information. You never know when you'll need to come back to some crucial piece of information, so you want to make this as easy to use as you can.

TIP: There are also online resources to help you organize your networking and job search activities. One we especially like is JibberJobber (www.jibberjobber.com), a free online organizer and relationship manager specifically for people in the midst of JobGetting.

Where the Jobs Are

With your information-tracking system in place, it's time to think about where the jobs are. When the economy is in a downturn, it's easy to just sit back, scan the want ads, and then say, "Well, there's nothing out there. What's the use in even trying?"

The fact is that there are always jobs out there and work to be done, even in the midst of downsizings and reorganizations and closings. People every day are changing positions or companies, new roles are being created constantly, and many companies are hiring in one department even as they lay off in another. Your task is to find these places and opportunities, and the key is to make maximum use of your resources and options.

There are four primary ways for you to find job openings:

- **Want ads/job networks/job boards:** Typically only about 20 percent of jobs are publicly posted in some form—listed in the want ads, in various job bulletins or job networks, and job boards. There will be a slightly higher percentage during labor shortages. This category includes Internet postings. More and more companies use the Internet to post openings when recruiting.

- **Executive search firms/recruiters:** Companies will pay for a search firm if they are in a hurry to fill a job, if the position involves some kind of high-demand specialty, or sometimes if it is an upper-level position. Our research indicates that less than 15 percent of new jobs are secured through some form of headhunter/recruiter.

- **Targeted direct cold calls:** This strategy involves targeting companies you'd like to work for and then presenting yourself. It takes self-confidence and initiative. Our research indicates that about 5 to 10 percent of people find new jobs using this strategy. Not many other career strategists talk about this strategy, which may be one of the reasons it pays off for some people.

- **Networking:** This is by far the single most effective strategy, at all levels and in all fields. It involves talking directly with people and asking for their help. Our research indicates that as much as 60 percent of new positions are secured through some form of networking. This figure increases if you include online networking as well.

We want your JobGetting strategy to involve all four sources: want ads or other postings, executive search firms, targeted cold calls/letters, and networking. But we urge you to devote your time to each strategy according to its likelihood of success for you. That means, for example, that you should spend roughly 20 percent of your time chasing down want ads, no more than 15 percent of your time talking with headhunters, and no more than 10 percent of your time making cold calls. Save the bulk of your time and energy for networking!

The following sections show how each strategy works.

Want Ads/Job Networks

You will want to study the newspaper and online ads at least once a week. You will also want to make use of appropriate business and professional periodicals and online journals in your field. When you see an opening that interests you, follow the Deems JobGetting Skills™ strategy described in chapter 8 when a name or company is listed. That means your application needs to start with some phone calls to learn as much as you can about the position *before* you decide whether to apply. Remember, it takes more energy and confidence to pick up the phone and call than it does to merely sit back and mail a letter! Decision makers look for people with energy and confidence.

If you see a position that interests you, but no company is listed (a "blind ad"), you might be able to figure out which of several companies it could be, especially if you're searching geographically. Ask yourself, "What are the companies in this area that might hire someone like this?" Check with your network to see who they think might have placed the ad, and ask whether they know of anyone who works in those companies. If a name is provided, follow up with that person for additional information.

Even if your networking turns up no leads or introductions, you can still go to the companies you believe might have placed the ad. Identify the key decision maker for your content area, make the contact, and introduce yourself. Let the person know you are looking for a position that matches the job title or description from the ad and would like to find time to talk in detail about how you might fit within their organization.

If your digging does not result in any names or company ideas, respond as other applicants will: Draft the best cover letter you can and send it along with your resume. That's about as much as you can do for now. Because blind ads are generally considered a long shot (and may be nothing more than a fishing trip on the part of the company, just to see who might be out there looking), do not invest much time or energy in these announcements.

Responding to Blind Ads with Cover Letters

Your cover letter is a key strategic document and deserves some added attention here. The cover letter needs to identify how you are aware of the position and then show how you meet the required qualifications. The body of your letter will then address each of the qualifications in the same order as listed in the ad. In your writing, keep your tone friendly but professional. Don't be afraid to let some of your personality shine through.

Here is an example of a cover letter for a blind ad that calls for someone with at least three years of management experience in data processing who is familiar with new operating systems, able to serve as project team leader, has a degree in computer science or a related field, and has experience managing others. Notice the general structure of the letter and the fact that the word "I" is used sparingly. Many people make two common mistakes that we want you to avoid:

- **Putting their most important information (their qualifications) into one long paragraph.** It's better to use bullet points because this makes it easier for the reader to see how you qualify. When information is simply included in a long paragraph, readers will do a quick scan and quite possibly will miss some of your key points.

- **Using too much "I."** Because the letter is about you, it's tough not to use "I" at least a couple of times. But starting several sentences and paragraphs with "I" can convey self-centeredness, which is not the message you want to get across. Look for ways to restructure sentences to minimize the use of "I."

Figure 7.3 is a sample cover letter.

Jennifer Wassau
1212 Meadow Lane
Oxford, IA 50422
(555) 666-7777   jenwassau@ldr.com

May 14, 2010

P.O. Box 123
The Tribune
Des Moines, IA 50333

Good morning,

Your ad in today's *The Tribune* announcing your search for an IT manager caught my attention. It appears my strengths and experiences match your identified needs and I would appreciate your consideration for this position.

The enclosed resume summarizes my background and abilities. Briefly, these include

- Bachelor of Science degree in computer science from MIT.
- More than five years of experience managing IT operations, with five direct reports and up to 75 indirect reports.
- Knowledgeable of new operating systems; member of a national users network helping the industry identify needs and research options, with an emphasis on social networking.
- Led three project teams to implement new systems, bringing projects in ahead of schedule and within budget.
- Professional...strong work ethic...most effective within high-performance work environments.

I am available at your convenience for a meeting in your office to talk in more detail about your specific job needs and how I might contribute to your organizational goals. Please contact me at the above phone number or by e-mail at jenwassau@ldr.com. I look forward to hearing from you soon!

Sincerely,

Jennifer Wassau

Figure 7.3: Sample cover letter responding to blind want ad.

TIP: Never use "Dear Sir/Madam" or "To Whom It May Concern" in your greeting. If you cannot identify a specific person, go with the company name, such as "Dear WorkLife Design." If you do not know the name of the company, use a simple "Good Morning" or "Greetings!" as your salutation.

Responding to "No Phone Calls" Ads

If an ad provides a name for people to contact, but states "no phone calls," you can do one of two things. First, see whether your network can provide an introduction to a key decision maker within that company. If yes, call and say something like this:

> *We have a mutual friend in Pam Lastname and Pam told me she thought you were looking for someone with my qualifications. If so, I'd like to take a few minutes to talk with you about what you need and how I might fit....*

Then continue with the Deems JobGetting Skills™ system, discussed in chapter 8.

If, however, your network can't provide an introduction, your only viable approach is to play their game and respond with a letter. Figure 7.4 is another example.

Remember, your cover letter must address the stated qualifications in the same order and using some of the same words, as printed in the job announcement. If no qualifications are provided, think through what the logical qualifications would be for this type of position. You can also look up similar positions online and see what others are looking for in this role.

Stating your qualifications clearly, and in the order presented in an ad, makes it very clear that you meet all of the basic qualifications and that your letter needs to go into the "let's interview" pile.

Responding Directly to a Decision Maker

If you are able to speak with a decision maker about the position before sending in your application (the ideal approach), your cover letter will be slightly different. Now you have a specific person's name and can refer to your conversation at the beginning of the letter. Your letter could look something like figure 7.5.

If you have found the position on the Internet, and the instructions tell you to submit your resume via e-mail, you will still prepare a cover letter. The note, however, will be much briefer. Just be sure the basics are still covered:

- Express your interest in the position.
- Thank them for their time on the phone (if applicable).
- Address the key qualifications you have.

Jason J. Smyth
5446 Watson Street
Greensboro, NE 68909
(402) 444-4444   JJsmyth21@msn.com

December 10, 2010

Dave Germane
CSR Manager
TellAll, Inc.
316 N. Forester Avenue
Lancey, MN 56565

Dear Mr. Germane,

Recently I learned of your search for a customer service representative. Your needs seem to match my own skills and experience very well, and I would appreciate your consideration for this position.

The enclosed resume highlights my background and abilities. Briefly, these include the following:

- Associate in Applied Science degree, with emphasis in communications.
- Successful CSR experience includes five years within a full-service call center, handling inbound calls and responding to customer concerns and questions.
- Develop quick rapport with even the most difficult of customers; excellent communication and interpersonal skills.
- Participated on project team to implement new phone system; assisted in troubleshooting the new system and training other CSRs on new equipment.
- Enthusiastic…professional…enjoy new challenges and frequently commended for providing the highest quality of service to customers.

TellAll is recognized as one of the major leaders in its field, and the opportunity to be part of the CSR team is very appealing. I'm looking forward to meeting you in the near future and talking in more detail about your specific job needs and how I can meet those needs.

Sincerely,

Jason J. Smyth

Figure 7.4: Sample cover letter responding to want ad that provides a contact name.

Emanuel "Manny" Rodriguez
17 Bolder Parkway, Apt. 8
Hedgegrove, PA 85355

April 16, 2010

Janice Krausmann
Operations Manager
Hedgegrove Plastics
1111 Amboy Blvd.
Hedgegrove, PA 85355

Dear Janice,

Thank you for taking the time this morning to talk with me about your second-shift production opening! The information you provided has confirmed my interest, and I would appreciate your consideration for this position.

As you suggested on the phone, I have enclosed a copy of my resume for your review. Briefly, my qualifications include the following:

- More than 7 years of experience in production environments; demonstrated ability to learn new skills quickly and to lead production efforts.
- Served as team lead for 8-member team and communicated with mangers to investigate and resolve performance problems.
- Handled supervisory duties in the absence of regular floor supervisor.
- Proposed several new process plans that were implemented and resulted in significant cost savings.
- Enthusiastic...strong work ethic...work effectively with diverse groups of people.

As I mentioned during our phone conversation, I've been caught up in the recent downsizing at Foxworth. Although I will miss my co-workers, I am looking forward to making similar contributions within an organization such as Hedgegrove Plastics. I'll be in touch with your office near the end of this week to see when it would be convenient to talk further. I look forward to meeting with you soon!

Sincerely,

Manny Rodriguez

Figure 7.5: Cover letter following a telephone conversation.

If the online announcement asks you to submit your resume through the company's Web site, you may find a place there to include a cover letter. If not, you may be able to create a cover letter as the first page of your resume. If the system allows for only the resume, simply submit it with no cover letter.

We'll describe the process in more detail in the next section, but it's worth mentioning here as well: Unless the system forces you to respond only with a resume, look for other ways to get in front of the decision maker. For example, you can send your resume to the HR department, but also think through who really needs to see your resume—who is the decision maker. There is no rule that prevents you from getting your piece of paper in front of the person who most needs to see it.

FINDING THE JOBS

When it comes to responding to ads, remember: For most fields, only about 20 percent of the available jobs will be listed in the want ads. This suggests two things:

- Not more than 20 percent of your JobGetting time should be devoted to exploring and responding to want ads or similar posted openings. If you are JobGetting full time, this works out to about one day of your JobGetting work week.

- You need to find out where the other 80 percent of the openings are. Fortunately, this is not difficult to do!

TIP: In addition to want ads, several job opening networks have developed in the past several years, including the Workforce Development departments within each state. These are another source of openings, and many of these announcements will never make it to the traditional want-ad section of your newspaper. In addition, many professional and craft fields have their own job networks and publications for posting openings. Respond to these as you would any other posted want ad: hopefully with a phone call first, followed by a strategically crafted cover letter and targeted resume.

Remember that you can check want ads either through area newspapers or online. If you have access to a computer and Internet service, using online tools to find ads can save you a great deal of time and aggravation because you can search by industry, job type, date, and location. You can make use of online newspapers or use an online help-wanted site that compiles newspaper ads into one searchable job bank. Sites include CareerBuilder, Monster.com, and Yahoo! HotJobs; and even sites like craigslist offer want-ad sections. We'll talk more about using the Internet later in this chapter.

Key point: If you only chase want ads, you will seriously limit your chances and opportunities—and you will extend the amount of time it takes to turn job hunting into JobGetting. However, you shouldn't exclude the want ads, either.

They are one of several resources for you to use, but plan to devote no more than one day a week to them.

HOW I PLAN TO USE WANT ADS AND OTHER POSTED ANNOUNCEMENTS

\
\
\
\
\
\

Executive Search Firms, Recruiters, and Placement Offices

Too many people want to believe that all they have to do is get in contact with the right executive search firm or recruiter and "They will find me the right spot."

NOT!

Executive search firms, headhunters, and recruiters make money by placing the right person in the right job. True, they are always looking for good people to present as candidates. However, if they do not have an opening on their books that calls for a person with your talents and abilities, they will not be very interested in talking with you or working for you.

There is also a difference between the various types of recruiting firms:

- **A retainer-based firm** is paid a retainer fee by the hiring company to do a search and present one or several viable candidates. Their success depends on their ability to bring the right person. Unless they have an actual contract to present someone like you, they are typically not interested in talking with potential candidates. Or they may talk with you and only add you to their database.

- **A contingency-based firm** is paid a fee only if their candidate is offered the position and accepts. These people are often referred to as "recruiters" because they uncover candidates and then attempt to "sell" these people to firms already on their client list. Sometimes it is a good fit, and sometimes not.

Sometimes recruiters mass mail candidates' resumes to potential employers hoping that some company responds. This can create a problem for you. If you have a contact who gets you into a company, but after the recruiter has sent your resume (usually unknown to you), the company will have to pay a fee to the recruiter if you are offered and accept a position. The result is that even though the company may want to talk with you, their interest may decrease if they have to "buy" you with a fee.

Our suggestion: Unless you know someone who works as a recruiter, or are conducting a national search and have a limited network, you are probably best advised to not focus on them in your Plan for Action. Instead, select only two or three headhunters to talk with and periodically keep in contact. They are one more resource for your Plan for Action, but they are not your primary resource.

For many levels of positions, a recruiter will not be appropriate, but a placement office might be. These are businesses that, like recruiters, attempt to match people with job openings their clients bring to them. The process is much the same as it is for a recruiter, in that you'll be invited for an interview with the placement staff, and if they have a current client they believe you would be a good fit for, they'll make the match or forward your name to the hiring organization. This may be another part of your strategy. Just keep in mind a few things:

- Never pay out of your own pocket for the service; reputable placement offices are paid by the hiring company, not the individual candidate.

- Ask to be kept informed concerning where they submit your resume so that you do not submit a duplicate on your own.

- Avoid placement offices that require you to work only through them in your job search; this is not in your best interest (it's in *their* best interest).

Using recruiters, search firms, or placement offices can be part of your total strategy, but be selective in choosing whom to work with and how to work with them. Identify two to three firms to work with, with particular focus on those that work most with people who do what you want to do, in the industry you are targeting.

Because fewer than 15 percent of available openings are filled this way, spend no more than 15 percent of your weekly time on this strategy.

HOW I PLAN TO USE EXECUTIVE SEARCH FIRMS, RECRUITERS, OR PLACEMENT OFFICES

_____

_____

_____

_____

_____

_____

NOTE: People sometimes ask us whether working with a temp agency to gain temporary employment is a good idea. This is an individual decision you will need to make based on your unique situation. There are temp agencies for executives, professionals, and just about every level of position you can imagine. Taking temporary employment can be a good strategy if you need some quick income, you want a chance to check out a variety of companies and expand your professional network, or you aren't sure yet just what direction you want your career to take. Do be cautious, though, especially if you are collecting unemployment or have a severance arrangement with your previous employer that would disappear when you begin earning a new income.

Targeted Direct Cold Calls

You will also want your Plan for Action to include the strategy of making cold calls on those targeted companies for which you would like to work. Approximately 5 to 10 percent of JobGetters land their next position through cold contacts.

First, compile a list of your preferred companies to work for (preferred for any reason—their reputation, location, and so on). Take some time to brainstorm: Which companies hire people who do what I want to do? Many people find it helpful to create an A list and a B list of organizations, based on some criteria they have set (for example, driving distance).

Use your network to see whether you can get an introduction to a key decision maker within any of those preferred companies. If you use a professional social networking site such as LinkedIn or Plaxo, this can be a convenient way of making connections to your target companies. If you can get an introduction, make your contact and present yourself as someone who really wants to work for that company. Be ready to tell why you want to work for that company and what you have to offer.

If your network can't provide an introduction, get the name of the decision maker involved in your particular area of expertise. Call and make an appointment, and present yourself as someone who really wants to work for that particular company.

You can use introductory statements like the following:

> *Of the 30 companies in this city that hire people like myself, your company, ABC Corporation, is in my opinion the number-one company. You have an outstanding product, have a reputation as one of the nation's best-managed corporations, and you help your employees be successful. This is the kind of company I'd like to be a part of, and I would appreciate the chance to talk with you about what I can bring to ABC Corporation.*

Here's another example:

> *A recent article in the* Daily Bugle *reported on your new pension administration operation. I have more than 10 years of experience in that field and have developed some systems for marketing that have been very successful. I'm in a career stage where I'm looking for a new challenge, and the challenge of being part of a team to start up such a division is really appealing. I'd like to have the chance to talk with you about your new operation and how I might be able to contribute.*

TIP: The daily newspaper, local business magazine, and online news sites can be another valuable resource for you. Flag articles referring to plans for expansion, reorganization, promotions, and so on: There may be new roles or empty positions available.

You may well be told that "we don't have any openings right now." If that's the case, thank them and explain that you did not expect that they would right now. But you wanted them to know what you do best, and that you are available in the event something unexpectedly comes open. Ask whether you can send them a copy of your resume and follow up with them again later.

If this organization is on your "A" list, find ways to stay in front of them regularly. Why? Eventually, a position will open up, and when it does, you want them to think about you!

Cold calling takes

- Self-confidence

- Self-awareness

- Energy

If you are like Terri—a rather shy introvert—cold calling can be stressful and feel uncomfortable, at least at first. Generally, though, people find that the more they do this, the easier and more comfortable it gets. If you simply cannot make yourself make the calls, try a "cold letter" instead. This letter is similar to a cover letter; however, you are not applying for a particular position. You simply want to present yourself to a decision maker. You might include a closing paragraph like this:

> *I don't expect that you would have an opening at this time. If, however, something unanticipated becomes available later this fall, I would appreciate you keeping me in mind. I'll stay in touch as well. Also, feel free to pass along my resume to others you think might have an interest—I'd appreciate that!*

Decision makers like to talk with people who have confidence, who know what they can contribute, and who have energy for the job. That's why cold calling can be an effective way to turn job hunting into JobGetting.

How I Can Use Targeted, Direct Cold Calling

Networking

Our experience and research have been consistent over the past several years: Your single best strategy in finding available positions is through your own personal network. More than 60 percent of new jobs are secured through some form of networking or word of mouth, and it's networking that allows you to tap into that "hidden" job market—the jobs that never get posted. This suggests that you need to devote at least 60 percent of your job search time to networking.

Here's how you do it:

Using your organizing system (note cards, PC database, and so on), generate a list of people you know, along with their contact numbers (phone, e-mail). Keep at it until you have a contact file of 25 to 100 people (or even more). Eventually, you will have a file of Primary Contacts (people you know personally as friends, co-workers, and so on) and Secondary Contacts (people to whom you are referred, and people you know but who are more distant acquaintances).

You can start developing your Network File even before you begin your intensive job search. When you begin your intensive job search, get in touch with your Primary Contacts and your main Secondary Contacts. Update them on your situation and ask for some of their time. *Assure them that you are not asking them for a job, but you would like their advice and help.* Try to get a brief face-to-face meeting, which may include a breakfast or lunch (your treat). That face-to-face time is better than simply a phone call or e-mail letting them know you are searching because it gets you out of the house and provides more opportunity for brainstorming and suggestions.

What to Say

Prepare yourself to summarize what you have to offer (your 30-second "elevator speech"). Start by reviewing the key strengths you identified in chapter 3, and use this to prepare a brief overview of what you have to offer and what you are looking for. This elevator speech should take no more than 30 seconds to say. Practice it until it sounds spontaneous and feels natural to you.

Have your elevator speech ready and use it appropriately depending on what your network contact wants or needs to know about you. There are two common questions people within your network are likely to ask you and your elevator speech may be the focus of your response:

- What are you looking for?
- How can I help you?

As you network, be ready to ask whether they know any people who might know of openings that call for a person with your skills and abilities. Be ready to explain why you are looking for a certain kind of position, why you know you will do it well, and what you consider to be your strengths. Also be ready to ask specifically for two or three names of people your contact knows that you can get in touch with:

> *Doug, as you're aware, there were 15 of us who were reorganized out of DEF Corporation. I enjoyed my time there and know I made many contributions. Now I'm looking for a position as (this or that) ...and I wonder if you know of any such openings...or if you know others who I should be talking with....*

Be well prepared for a question that you'll get dozens of times: *What are you looking for?* Be as specific as you can while still communicating it within one or two minutes, at most. In preparing this, try out a variety of ways to say what you are looking for.

Here are some quick examples:

- I'm looking for a leadership position within x type of company, where I can use my skills in project management, strategic planning, and enhancing performance. I'd prefer a company that....

- I'm looking for a position where I can use my management skills in an office environment....

- I'm not sure what I'm looking for exactly. But I know I want to continue using my skills in x, y, and z, and I really want a work environment that....

The work you already did on your resume and in thinking about your best work environment will help you create this statement. Then, *practice it!* You want to be very clear in your own mind about what you plan to say, but you also want this to sound natural and spontaneous—not like something you just memorized last night. Practice until it feels very natural to you. Depending on your career direction, and with whom you are speaking, your response might vary slightly.

Make use of secondary contacts—people you don't know well, or maybe don't know at all but were provided an introduction to by someone else. When contacting a secondary contact, you can say something like this:

> *Robin, our mutual friend Travis suggested I contact you. I was one of 15 who were reorganized out of DEF Corporation, and I'm looking for a position as (this or that). Travis said you have a lot of insight into that*

*field and that you might be willing to give me some reactions to my Plan for
Action. Could we spend 15 to 20 minutes together next week?*

TIP: Do not ask a contact for a job. Most people want to help, and if they do not
have a job for you, they may be embarrassed or uncomfortable. Instead of giving
you information, they may simply deny you a chance to meet. Your task is to put
them at ease and to assure them that you merely want their advice and help.

Assure them that you are not asking them for a job, nor do you expect them
to have one for you. You are seeking their advice and help in reviewing your
Plan for Action, perhaps looking over your resume, and providing additional
contacts. If they do know of an opening, trust that they will tell you if they
think it is appropriate. If they tell you of an opening, ask whether they know
the name of the key decision maker and if you can use your contact's name
when contacting this person.

Your Agenda

Your agenda for meeting with either a primary or secondary contact needs to
be carefully thought out so that you make the best use of your time. Write out
what you want to accomplish; list agenda items if it will help. Here is one way
to approach a networking meeting:

1. Such meetings usually begin with small talk—to bridge the past to the
    present or establish rapport from your primary contact to your secondary
    contact. When the person asks "What can I do for you?" the chit-chat is
    over.

2. Be ready to talk about what you're looking for, your major strengths,
    examples of contributions, and what you believe you can bring to a new
    situation. Just like preparing for an interview, anticipate the kinds of
    questions you might be asked. Present your resume, give the person
    time to review it (or send it to him or her ahead of time), and be ready to
    answer questions the person might have.

3. You may need to clarify why you left your previous employer. The infor-
    mation you provide will be very similar to how you answer the interview
    question, "Why are you available now?"

4. If appropriate, mention your target companies. "Some of the companies
    I'm really interested in are…. I'm wondering if you know key people
    within those organizations that I could talk with."

5. Share your JobGetting Plan for Action (see chapter 8). Ask for feedback,
    advice, or other information that might be helpful to you.

6. Before you leave, ask for the names of several people you can contact who might know of organizations looking for someone with your experience, skills, and abilities. Ask for permission to use the person's name when you contact these new people.

7. Thank the person for his or her time and let the person know you really appreciate the help he or she has provided!

After the Meeting

Keep a record each time you contact someone from your network, including the kind of information provided and the results of the information. Create other appropriate follow-up plans, and create new cards or files as you get new introductions. There will be some people in your network that you'll want to stay in regular contact with, so schedule on your calendar when you will do so. Also, continue to add new people to your network file as you make new acquaintances.

And when the day comes that you accept a new position, you want to let these people know and thank them for their help during your search. A letter tends to work better than a phone call because the receiver has something physical to hold on to and look at. It's always nice to read a letter that says "thank you!"

Your network will remember you for about two to three weeks. It's not that they want to forget you, it's just that you are not their main responsibility. If nothing has happened after you've contacted your network, contact them again. We continually have candidates report to us that it was only after the second or third or fourth contact with a specific person that the person said, "Hey, great that you called—let me tell you what I heard yesterday!"

When a contact says, "I think there's an opening at XYZ Corporation, and Jim James is the person to talk with," find out as much as you can about both XYZ Corporation and Jim James. Then call, following the Deems JobGetting Skills System™ outlined in chapter 8.

Overcoming Objections to Networking

Sometimes job hunters hesitate to network, which might be why they stay job hunters rather than JobGetters! They think they are imposing, or they don't want to bother others, or they don't find it easy or aren't sure what to say. We've found over the years that

- Many people enjoy networking, particularly if they give themselves a few practice tries with it or if they are extroverts. Remember to stay focused on your main fields of interest.

- Some people do not enjoy networking and find it to be hard work. Find ways to make it easier for yourself by thinking of it as a game or challenge. Start with people you are most comfortable with and then continue to expand your network.

- Some people view networking as intruding on others. In addition, because you can't always anticipate what will happen when you're networking, some people may find it stressful. Remember that most people enjoy helping others and that, to them, networking is not intruding. Trust that, if a person feels it is intrusive, they will decline to meet with you.

- Still others may presume that the people in their network either won't know anything of value, or won't take time, or won't be available, or some other negative conclusion. Don't make that decision for others! Go ahead and ask for their help and let them decide if and how they can help you. Most people we've worked with are surprised at how willing to help others are, especially if they've been in the same JobGetting spot as you.

- Finally, some people find it difficult to use the phone. That's fine; make ample use of e-mail, then, or simply head over to where your network person is to set up a time to meet and talk further.

THINGS TO REALIZE ABOUT NETWORKING

Most people want to help. Most people enjoy helping. If you decide not to call someone, you have just made a decision for that person. It's better to call the person, ask for help, and let the person decide for himself or herself. People like to help for a variety of reasons:

- Most people have an urge to help others.

- Some get an ego boost out of the role of helping and advising you.

- Many may have been in the same place you are now and quickly identify with your situation.

- If you are well prepared and informed about your particular field, they stand to learn from the sharing of ideas and information.

If you find networking to be difficult, just keep at it. You'll learn. Talk with others to see how they handled networking in their own JobGetting. Remember to make use of people you know through community groups, recreational activities, professional associations, online networks, and even church or your local fitness center.

It may help to think of it like this: You don't know, right now, how you will find out about your next position nor who will tell you initially about it. You don't even know whether your next position is open today. What you are trying to do is position yourself so that, when your next position becomes open, someone near that position will think of you. Networking is a key way of helping to make that happen. Talk with everyone you can about what you are looking for.

Will everyone you want to talk to, want to talk with you? Of course not. But let them decide that; don't decide for them. You are likely to be surprised at how helpful your networking will be when you approach it confidently, persistently, and with a clear sense of what you want.

MY PLAN FOR NETWORKING

Using the Internet

A recent study of human resource managers shows that 70 percent of those surveyed use the Internet as a recruiting tool. Another study notes that upwards of 90 percent of recent college grads use the Internet to do a significant part of their job searching. With this kind of use, you can't afford not to make use of the Internet.

Over the past several years, we have seen a steady migration away from newspaper want ads to Internet sources—for job seekers, human resource offices, and recruiters. Because of the vastness of this global network, there are no reliable statistics for the proportion of openings that are filled this way. Nevertheless, you will want to include the Internet as part of your strategy, whether it's for company research, finding openings, or making use of an online social network such as Facebook or LinkedIn. There are a number of ways the Internet can be useful to your JobGetting:

- **Researching organizations:** Before applying for any specific position—and particularly before an interview—you want to learn as much as you can about the organization: goals, mission, values, work environment, products and services, key decision makers, and so on. If it's a public company, click on the Investor Relations button and you will find who's who within the organization. You can learn a great deal by visiting an organization's Web site or running the company name through a search engine to see what comes up.

- **Researching people:** There will likely be times when you want to learn more about a particular decision maker, and the Internet can help you here as well. Searching a person's name can give you valuable information about a decision maker's history, interests, and past accomplishments. Search carefully, though; you want to be sure you are getting information about the correct person!

- **Identifying openings:** There are two different ways you can use the Internet to help you find openings. If you are interested in working for a particular company, you can go directly to its Web site and see what openings are listed on the career or employment pages. The company may also provide a way for you to submit your resume directly to its application database.

  You can also find openings through job Web sites such as Monster.com or CareerBuilder.com. Recent estimates showed upwards of 35,000 job-posting sites on the Internet. Some of these offer a wide range of jobs and locations; others have a more defined focus on types of positions, locations (such as international work), or levels of positions. If you are seeking an industry-specific position, use a site that focuses on that industry. In general, however, you want to make use of two kinds of sites: a "want ad" site that simply posts ads from classified sections of U.S. newspapers, and a site that includes ads that are not posted in newspapers. The best sites allow you to search by specific job titles, location, or other keywords.

- **Exploring salary information:** Part of your research needs to include finding the average and range of wages or salaries for particular kinds of positions, in different parts of the country or internationally. This will help when you are eventually asked to give your salary requirements. Numerous Web sites can provide this kind of information. Some sites, such as www.salary.com, the HomeFair calculator at www.homefair.com (click on the salary calculator button under Moving), and www.payscale. com also give you a salary calculator to help you figure cost-of-living adjustments in different parts of the country or to calculate relocation costs.

- **Networking:** Whether it's through e-mail or a social networking site such as Facebook or LinkedIn (or any number of other such sites), the Internet can be a valuable networking tool. When using a social networking site, do exercise some caution: Some sites are focused on particular professions or professional interests, whereas others are purely social. Choose carefully. And if you already make use of Facebook or MySpace, and in the past have not been too concerned over what you post there, now is a good time to make sure your pages are blocked from all but your closest friends. As part of today's selection process, many employers will search a job candidate's name online—and they will not be impressed with those pictures from last year's beach party or cute nicknames others use for you!

- **Finding emerging fields of employment:** A number of sites periodically report on studies of current and future job trends. You can check out your state's Workforce Development site to learn what the "hot" fields are in your area.

- **Improving job hunting skills:** In addition to the thousands of sites available to identify job openings, many sites have useful JobGetting information, such as interviewing dos and don'ts. Like anything on the Internet, however, there is a mix of good and bad information. Select one or two sites that have trustworthy information from reliable sources. JIST Publishing, the nation's leading publisher of career-related resources, has many excellent books and videos, and you can get daily job hunting tips from its blog at http://jistjobsearchandcareer.blogspot.com/.

In addition, you can post your resume to online databases that employers and recruiters seeking candidates use. Many of these include an e-mail alert of some sort to let you know when it has found a position in which you might be interested.

Be careful, though, of online job scams, which are aplenty. Posting your resume on some sites may get you calls from people wanting to set you up in your own home business (for a large fee, of course) or "investment opportunities" if you provide some up-front money to them. There are also companies that actively solicit resumes and then try to "help" you with your job search (again, for a large fee). These can be especially difficult to spot until you're in their office: People post their resume and then get a call from someone wanting them to come in for an interview but they will be vague as to what the position is. If you set the appointment and go in, you may face a hard-sell situation where they try to bully you into signing a contract with them for several thousand dollars (and they'll not do anything beyond what you can do for yourself, anyway).

The point is this: Make good use of all the job search tools and resources online, but also take appropriate precautions when talking with others. If you receive a call about your posted resume, make sure the person is from a legitimate company and has a legitimate opening.

The Internet can be a key tool to assist in your JobGetting—if you use it strategically. It can also, however, turn into a time waster for you, distracting you from taking other more active actions needed to turn job hunting into JobGetting. Use it carefully, and budget the amount of time you spend online. Don't use it so much that you avoid talking directly with people.

TIP: Take a look at your e-mail address. Does it help you present a professional image? If you use a name like hotbabe or dunkindave, set up a new e-mail address that you will use specifically for your JobGetting. That's a good idea regardless of the name you presently use because it will help you keep JobGetting e-mails separate from the other messages you generally receive.

How Will You Turn Job Hunting into JobGetting?

Turning job hunting into JobGetting takes time, energy, and a thoughtful approach to how you will identify and respond to openings and opportunities. Create a purposeful strategy and make use of as many resources and options as you can. For effective JobGetting, be sure to include the following:

1. Carefully design your strategies using *all* resources, including

     - Want ads/job networks

     - Headhunters/recruiters/placement offices

     - The Internet

     - Targeted cold calls

     - Networking

2. Keep yourself on a schedule and plan to devote several hours each day, Monday through Friday, to your JobGetting activities. If you are used to keeping a calendar, keep doing it. Decide what time you'll start work, when you'll make calls, what day of the week to go through want ads or search online, and so on. Then write these activities into your calendar and on your Plan for Action. By scheduling your time, you will be less likely to let outside interruptions affect your work.

3. Have someone, besides a family member, with whom you can regularly report your efforts and get realistic feedback concerning your efforts. This will help you stay on schedule by giving you someone to whom you are accountable. Do not use family members for this, however. Spouses are most useful for hugs and encouragement and can't always be brutally honest with you when you need it.

4. Set specific goals for yourself each day or each week and *write them down.* Also take time each week to evaluate your results and see what changes you need to make. If the weekly goals are not met, evaluate: What barriers got in your way? What steps can you take next week to ensure that you will reach your goals?

NOTE: Remember, YOU are in charge of this project to turn job hunting into JobGetting! It's your job to determine your schedule. You strategize about ways to get in front of decision makers. You plan, carry out, and evaluate your action steps. Give this project the time, attention, and care it deserves.

If you use all possible resources for identifying openings and approach your search with energy and drive, you will become a JobGetter!

HOW LONG WILL IT TAKE?

It is our experience that the higher the level, the more time it takes to locate that correct "fit" between unmet needs and your abilities and qualities. The competition is less in upper levels, but decision makers are more demanding in finding that fit.

What we consistently find is if you are getting interviews and you believe the interviews are going well, it is only a matter of time before that right fit occurs. You are emerging at the top of the pool of candidates for that kind of position. How much more time will it take? It varies, and there is no real way to predict how long.

What we do know is the more time and energy you put into this each week, the sooner you will see results. Position yourself, organize yourself, use all available options to identify openings and opportunities, and present yourself as enthusiastically as you can.

BILL'S STORY

Bill was the athletic director of a private four-year college and really enjoyed his work. But then budget cuts hit hard and he had to look for a new position.

In higher education, the normal procedure is to look through the listings in professional journals and then follow a strict procedure. That wasn't Bill's idea. Instead, he got on the phone and started calling his friends and acquaintances who held similar positions in other colleges and universities—networking. He turned up several openings across the nation. Most of those openings, he noticed, were not listed in any of the higher education professional journals.

Bill started researching the openings and narrowed his list to five colleges and universities. Then he studied the Web sites of each. He narrowed his list to three. As part of his research, he found the name and phone number of the institutions' presidents. He picked up the phone and put in a call directly to each president. His message: "My name is Bill Lastname, and several friends have told me you're looking for a new athletic director. If that's correct, I'd like a chance to talk with you to see if what you need doing at your college is what I do best." All three returned his call. The first president was

(continued)

(*continued*)

straightforward and told him a decision had already been made. That left two.

When Bill got through to the other presidents, he began, "I understand you have an opening for the athletic director's position." Both said yes, and both said something like, "Go ahead and send in your resume and we'll take a look at it."

Bill said yes, he could do that, but he wasn't going to clutter up the president's desk if what the president was looking for in an athletic director wasn't what Bill did best. The conversations continued. At one college the president said he needed someone to maintain the program. But Bill is a developer, not a maintainer. That left one.

And that's where Bill is today. Would he have the job if he had followed the traditional procedure? Maybe. "But I know I got the job because I showed the main decision maker what I could get accomplished. And it was what he wanted to get accomplished."

"The road to success is always *under construction."*
—*Cavett Robert*

CHAPTER 8

WHAT IS THE DEEMS JOBGETTING SKILLS™ SYSTEM?

What do you do when you hear of an opening that really interests you? *Job hunters* write a cover letter and send it with a resume to the personnel office, and then sit back and wait.

That will not be your strategy!

Job "hunting" is not your goal. "JobGetting" is your goal.

The best strategy is to learn, practice, and implement the five-step Deems JobGetting Skills™ System. It begins when you uncover a position that interests you.

In this chapter, you'll learn the five steps and how to implement them. This system is a proactive approach to turning job hunting into JobGetting. Based on time-tested concepts of career design, the system comes out of research, personal experience, and learning what does and does not work—the hard way. We've revised and improved it over 20 years based on the experiences of people just like you with whom we work, and feedback from decision makers in all industries.

This system is not what people are taught in college, nor what they read about in most job search books. Maybe that's why it works so well. But it does take extra time, energy, self-knowledge, and confidence.

Before going any further, stop and think for a moment. What is the difference between "hunting" and "getting"? Would you rather hunt or get? If you prefer to GET (and who wouldn't?), this system will work for you. It has probably helped you already, if you've caught the significance of the single word change. By changing job hunting to JobGetting, most people begin to think differently: They have more energy, and are more in control of themselves and more eager to get to the task at hand.

Will it work for your field? Yes! We have coached people to use the Deems JobGetting Skills™ System in just about every field: finance, insurance, the professions, media, manufacturing, government, retail, publishing, healthcare, and education. And we've found it's as relevant today as it was 20 years ago when we first started developing it.

As you read through the next several pages, you will realize that the JobGetting Skills system asks you to take an entirely different approach from what you may have been taught in the past. It starts with a simple difference: Before even applying for a position, *you find out as much as you can about the position to see if you are interested in doing what needs to be done.*

And it works! It works so well that many people who follow the system just matter-of-factly know they will be a finalist for every position for which they want to be considered! Of course, they don't apply for as many positions as does the typical job hunter. But then, why waste time and energy on something that you don't really want in the first place?

Things to Know Before You Start

You need to know three things before you learn the system:

- **The system works for all kinds of positions.** It can work for a fry cook's job just as well as it works for an executive vice president's position. This system is designed so that you can talk to decision makers about what needs to get done. From that discussion, you'll decide how best to position yourself as you make your application.

- **Not all managers and decision makers like the system.** About 9 percent of managers who've heard us describe the system in detail report they would not take the time for anyone who attempted to use it on them. Less than 5 percent of CEOs report to us that they would not let anyone talk to them about a position who follows this system. But that leaves more than 90 percent of managers and more than 95 percent of CEOs who report that they will give the time to people with enough confidence to follow this system. Managers and CEOs have reported to us that they are, in fact, often waiting for someone to use this kind of approach with them because it says a great deal about the person's interest, energy, and work ethic.

- **This system takes time and energy.** You will spend a great deal of time exploring a position before you decide to apply and before you ever send them anything. In the process, however, you will begin thinking how you would handle the responsibilities of the job that interests you.

In fact, most people who follow these steps begin "working" on the job even before they have a formal interview for the job.

The Five JobGetting Steps

When you hear of a position that interests you—whether from a friend, the newspaper, the Internet, or networking—be ready to take these steps:

- Step 1: Research the position.
- Step 2: Research the organization.
- Step 3: Evaluate your strengths and interests.
- Step 4: Design your positioning strategy.
- Step 5: Implement!

The following sections look more closely at each of these.

Step 1: Research the Position

When you hear of a position that interests you, for any reason, **contact the person who has the authority to hire you!** That's really the only person you want to get in front of. You tell the person, for example, that you understand he or she may have a position open for an accountant (or a receptionist, a warehouse clerk, or whatever the position is), and if so, you'd like to talk about their needs in detail. How do you find out who has the authority to hire you? Hopefully your source of information about a possible opening provided the key person's name and direct phone number. If not, you can still find out who to talk with through one of several different approaches.

Find the Information

You might first try contacting the company and simply asking the person who answers the telephone. For example, "I understand there may be an opening for an accountant and I'd like to know who will be the decision maker in the hiring process." You might get a name and title. Or you might simply be referred to someone in personnel or human resources. If so, thank them and hang up. Remember: Human resources and personnel offices are generally there to screen you, not to make the hiring decision (unless, of course, the position is actually within HR).

Another option is to go to the company's Web site. If it is a public company, look for the link to Investor Information or some similar label. On the new page you will probably find a link to Management, which lists the key executives and their areas of responsibility. You can also look at the Press

Releases link to see who is mentioned in recent press releases. The Press Releases page will also tell you what the company wants the public to know about them.

The local chamber of commerce or business association may also publish a list of local companies that includes key leaders within each organization. If it is a private or family-owned company, it may not be as easy to find the list of executives. But try it anyway. Be sure and look at the Press Releases section to see what names are listed and why. You may be able to identify the exact person you need to talk with.

The Internet may also help you find the information you need. Web sites such as www.hoovers.com and www.business.com provide various kinds of business intelligence through their directories and business search engines.

Make Contact

Your next task is to consider who might supervise the position. You may come up with a department head, division manager, or CEO, depending on the size and type of organization. Call the company to find out the name of the person in this position. Follow up with a second call at a later time, asking for the person by name. Generally, this will get you through, and you can then find out whether this person is indeed the decision maker or whether it is someone else. They'll let you know if there is someone better to talk to.

As a general rule, start high and let them direct you to the right person. After all, if you talk with vice president Tish A. and she says, "No, talk with the IT manager because he makes the final decision," and you tell the IT manager, "Vice president Tish A. asked me to talk with you about...," you'll get lots more attention.

You can talk with this decision maker over the phone, via e-mail, or in person. Whichever way you choose, have your questions ready before you make your contact. In this first step you are trying to find out as much about the position as you can, so that you can determine the following:

- Whether the company needs someone who has the skills and experience you have

- Whether you would like to have that position, in that particular organization

Many people are nervous about this step. Remind yourself what you are trying to do:

- Get your name across to the decision maker for the first time.

- Learn more about the position than other candidates will know.

- Decide whether this is a position you want to go after.

Say you get a decision maker on the phone. Then what? What if the person hesitates or says something like "Well, go ahead and mail in your resume and if we're interested we'll call you"? Be ready with a response that shows your determination to talk further and your interest:

> *Yes, I can do that. But I don't want to waste your time reviewing my resume if what you need doesn't involve what I do best.*

Most decision makers are not accustomed to having people contact them who are ready to talk about "What I do best." This will usually pique their interest, and they will want to hear what you have to say. Be ready!

The decision maker may well say, "Well, go ahead…tell me what you do best." That's your invitation to talk. Be ready to talk about your three areas of strength, with an example of a major accomplishment for each strength. Think ahead, and have those examples ready before you place the call. Select examples that will be familiar to the decision maker and apply to his or her company.

Also be ready with your own questions. Basically, you want to find out as much as you can about the position, which includes responsibilities, key functions, reporting relationships, major tasks to get accomplished, and so on. You might ask questions like these:

> *It would help me if you could describe the general duties and responsibilities of this position.*
>
> *Could you explain this…in more detail?*
>
> *What are the things that you need to get accomplished in the first year? In the next several months?*
>
> *What are the qualities you're looking for in the person who will fill this position?*
>
> *Why is the position vacant?*
>
> *What are the biggest challenges I would be facing in this position?*
>
> *In your job description, you mentioned leading a new team. It would help me if you could explain that in more detail.*
>
> *You mentioned that the job involves reorganizing the customer service efforts. I've been a key person in the reorganizations of three companies, including*

continuous improvement efforts directed toward customer satisfaction. Is this the kind of experience you're looking for?

If the decision maker likes what he or she hears, you will be asked a number of questions. What you will notice is that the phone call has turned into a relaxed, informal "interview" about what the company needs to get done and how you think you can get it done. Before the conversation ends, the decision maker may ask you one major question: "Why do you want to move and why are you available now?" Be ready with your answer!

Close your conversation, which, if the decision maker is interested in you, may take as long as an hour. If you're interested in the position, tell him or her! You can say something like this:

> *From your description, the position sounds like the kind of challenge I'm looking for. I'd appreciate a copy of your annual report and job description. Let me think about this some more and contact you again if I have further questions."*

By now you have gathered some important information about what the position involves and whether it needs someone with the skills and experiences you have. Before making your decision to pursue or not pursue the position, complete the next step.

OVERCOMING VOICE MAIL

In this day of voice mail, you may need to be persistent in reaching the decision maker. Keep at it! As a general rule, we suggest you make three to five tries to connect with that person, being sure to leave your name and a return phone number each time you call. One of your goals in making these calls is simply to get your name across to the decision maker. If you can do that only via voice mail, you will still have accomplished that goal. And that is something most other candidates will not have done.

If after the fifth call there is still no response, you will need to decide whether to pursue the position anyway, or move on to another opportunity. Remember, persistence usually pays off.

Step 2: Research the Organization

While continuing to research the position, you can begin to research the organization. To do this you can do the following:

- Ask the decision maker to send you a copy of the annual report or other pertinent material about the company (if it's not available online).

- Use the Internet to research the organization. Go to the organization's Web site and explore as many links as you can. Be sure to click on the Investor Relations links as well as the Press Releases link. Read the press releases and find out what the company is bragging about. Google some of the organization's leaders and learn more about them, also.

- Use your network (both offline and online, at LinkedIn or a similar social networking site) to find someone already in the company. See what they think of the company—its pros and cons.

In general, you want to know the following:

- The organization's history

- The organization's products or services

- The new products or services that have come online in the past, and what may be projected for the future

- Mergers or acquisitions the organization may have been involved in or is anticipating

- The organization's locations

- What it's like to work within the organization

- The key people within the organization

Your task is to find out as much as you can about the organization—and then decide whether you would like to be part of it.

REASONS YOU WANT TO WORK THERE

If you decide you'd like to be part of the organization, write out, in detail, at least five reasons why you want to work for that particular organization:

1. _____

_____

_____

2. _____

_____

_____

3. _____

_____

_____

4. _____

_____

_____

5. _____

_____

_____

As you research the organization, continue researching the position as time allows before the position's closing date. You do this by re-contacting the person who has the authority to hire you. In these subsequent contacts you are gathering more detailed information about the person's needs. You still have not decided whether you want the position, and you need to know as much as you can about what they need to have done. If what they need doing involves what you do best (and what you most enjoy doing), it appears there may be a fit.

We've referred to these questions earlier in this chapter, but they bear repeating. They are key questions you need answered in order to decide whether this is likely to be a good fit for you:

> *What are the major goals you would want me to accomplish during the first six months? The first year?*

> *What are the challenges I might encounter during the first six months? The first year?*

> *In your job description, you mentioned leading a new team. It would help me if you could explain that in more detail.*

You can also ask questions that continue to show you off and highlight your past accomplishments:

> *Before, when I've encountered something similar to that problem, I asked the team to identify possible solutions, we explored each one, and decided on our course of action. Are those actions similar to the approach you're looking for?*

> *From my experience in dealing with team success, I found that it took three major resources: a system to analyze the makeup of our team, an option to reformulate the team, and time to develop a real sense of "team." Are these resources available for this project to be successful?*

> *One of the ways I've led groups is to be clear in my expectations, have daily huddles, and be sure everyone gets praised for their contributions. Does this kind of approach fit your organization?*

Continue to research the position until you are sure you either want the job or don't want it.

NOTE: If, as you research the position and the organization, you like what you hear and find, you are likely to begin thinking about how you would do that job, even before you've formally applied for it. Congratulations! That will come through as you continue to talk with the decision maker. The more you can think about how you would handle that job, the more your enthusiasm will grow—and the more you're on the road to turning job hunting into JobGetting.

Step 3: Evaluate Your Strengths and Interests

After you've explored the position and the company, you need to stop, evaluate, and make a decision. Does the job call for what you do best and most enjoy doing? Will the workplace environment enable you to be your best? Do you want the job or not? One way to evaluate the position is to chart it out, listing your criteria for selecting a position and how this opportunity fits your criteria. If you're researching more than one opportunity at a time, compare them.

The following worksheet is an example of a way to compare the companies.

My Criteria	Company A	Company B	Company C
Duties/ responsibilities			
My management style and the company culture			

(continued)

(continued)

My Criteria	Company A	Company B	Company C
Use of what I do best/ what I most enjoy doing			
Location, and so on			
Compensation package			

If you decide what you do best isn't what the company really needs, tell the decision maker. You can say something like this:

> *I appreciate the time and interest you've shown me. But as I look at my notes, it seems what I do best is not what you're looking for. And I don't want to take up any more of your time. It would help me if I can describe for you what I do best, and perhaps you know of some organization in our area who needs someone like me.*

If the decision maker likes what he or she has heard, you will be asked to describe what you are looking for. Be ready. Also, be prepared to be introduced to another decision maker in the company who might be looking for someone exactly like you.

If there is no further interest on their part, bring closure. You might ask the decision maker whether he or she knows of any other decision maker who might need someone with your strengths and experience.

Finally, send a thank-you letter. Remember, anyone with whom you come into contact may be a potential member of your network and might, in fact, lead you to your next position. So be sure to send a note to anyone who has helped you in some way.

Step 4: Design Your Positioning Strategy

You've researched the position and concluded that what the company needs doing is exactly what you do best. In fact, it's something you get excited about doing, and you do it very well. In other words, you want the position!

Now what? You need to develop a plan to position yourself as a top candidate. Start with the following:

- **Contact the person again.** Tell them you want the position. In fact, you want to be considered their top candidate! After all, you don't want to be considered anything less than their top candidate, do you?

- **Simply ask the question,** "What can I bring to help you make a decision?"

Chances are the person will ask to see your resume, and of course you'll want to provide that. Take time, though, to look at your resume with this specific position in mind, and make whatever small changes might be needed so that the resume is targeted for this position.

Your positioning plan needs to go beyond the resume, however. What is your strategy beyond the resume? How can you keep your name in front of the decision maker, even as that person is reviewing other resumes? This is all part of your positioning, and it might include a contact to follow up on your resume, asking someone in your network to make a call on your behalf (if someone in your network knows the decision maker), and so on.

Take time to actually write down what steps you will take, now that you have decided to go after this position. Once this plan is made, you are ready for Step 5.

Step 5: Implement!

You've researched the position and the organization and know what they need matches with what you do best. You know you want the position, and you've designed your positioning strategy. Now it's time to implement that strategy.

1. **Assemble your application package according to the instructions of the person who has the authority to hire you.** If this includes your resume, be sure it is targeted to this position! Remember to carefully craft your cover letter as well, to direct the decision maker's attention to what he or she most needs to know about you.

2. **Deliver your application package in person, if at all possible.** As you deliver your package, have one more question to ask, or comment to make, that shows you already have been thinking about how you will handle the new position. This also creates a reason for the decision maker to contact you again if he or she is not available in person. If you cannot deliver your application in person, send it via e-mail or regular mail—or both.

3. **Follow up!** Now is not the time to just sit at home waiting for them to invite you in for more conversation. Wait two or three days for them to receive your application package; then call again to be sure it arrived. Have another good question ready for them. Go ahead and ask when a good time would be to sit down and talk in person about the position. Look over the other activities that you included in your positioning strategy, and stay on track with your plan.

While you're waiting, continue pursuing other positions as well. No matter how much of a sure thing a position looks like, you want to be continuously seeking out other opportunities as well. Remember, part of what you want is to give yourself choices, and you want to keep after other positions right up until you are ready to sign that new contract.

What if you go through all this and they don't hire you? Lots has happened. You have gained a new network of people who know you and are probably very impressed with you. Tell them again what you are looking for. Then ask for their help: "It will really help me find a position where I can make a significant contribution if you would share with me names of some of your contacts in other companies."

Listen. Ask for phone numbers. And ask whether you can use the person's name when you contact those referrals. Most will say "yes."

THE JOBGETTING SKILLS SYSTEM WORKS!

Yes, you're right: This system takes a lot more time, energy, and confidence than merely sitting back and mailing out letters or only responding to ads. But it works! And that's the difference.

This strategy is an important part of positioning yourself for the position you want. And it is a strategy that's not easy for all people. When Terri was experiencing her job loss, she found this system very difficult to follow because her personality is more introverted. She quickly discovered, though, that once she had done this a few times and had created something of a script for herself that felt natural, it was actually fun to do. Not everyone was willing to talk with her, but many were, and the information they provided helped her target her resume and letters and more effectively position herself for the interviews.

It works. Try it. Don't tell us it won't work if you haven't tried it. Don't decide that people will be bothered if you call them (let them make that decision; don't make it for them!). And try it several times. Sometimes people have to try it several times before their comfort level is high enough that they come through with the confidence that gets the decision maker's attention.

Formulating Your Plan for Action

Now it's time to develop your strategy—your Plan for Action. The more you put in writing, and even assign dates for completion, the easier it will be to keep on schedule.

People are far more likely to achieve their goal when they write down what they want to accomplish (the Objective), how they plan to accomplish it (the Strategy), and when they want to have it accomplished by (the Completion Date).

For example, one of your objectives for this week might be to make initial contact with the operations vice president at XYZ, Inc. Your strategies might include reviewing what you know about this person and XYZ, Inc., talking with this person about her needs, and hopefully arranging for a face-to-face meeting. And you want to have this completed by Thursday!

Or perhaps you think you'd love a job in that new store just a few blocks from where you live. Your goal is to get the name of the store manager or sales manager and make initial contact with that person. Your strategy will include getting the person's name and contact information and then placing a call to them to discuss their needs. From this, you'll put together a targeted resume and cover letter and deliver it on Tuesday.

You can use the following worksheet to get started on your own Plan for Action.

MY PLAN FOR ACTION

GOAL: To find the place where I can be most FULLY PRODUCTIVE and FULLY SATISFIED at the same time.

Objective	Strategies	Completion Date

_____

_____

_____

_____

_____

_____

_____

_____

_____

_____

Complete a weekly action plan for yourself. At the end of each week, review your actions to see what you achieved, what needs to be addressed next week, and what (if anything) prevented you from accomplishing your objectives. Some people like to create their plans first thing on Monday mornings and then review them late in the day on Friday. Others prefer doing both on the same day—reviewing what they did during the week and using that as the basis for the next week's plan. Whichever method you use, be disciplined in your use of the plan. Set specific and challenging (but realistic) objectives for yourself, implement your plan, and evaluate and refine.

Final Thoughts

An effective JobGetting strategy takes time and energy. You may find yourself asking, "How do I keep up my energy, particularly after nothing seems to be happening?"

First of all, if you are out talking to people, something _is_ happening! The only difficulty, from your perspective, is that you don't know exactly what is taking place as people talk to other people. One of the things we know is that if you're out talking with people, you're not sitting at home feeling sorry for yourself. And that's important.

Second, here are some things you can do to help maintain that energy, drive, and enthusiasm. These suggestions come from the experience of those with whom we've worked—people who have been right where you're at now. You may have already done some of these things after reading the earlier sections in this book. If you haven't done them yet, now is the time to start!

- If you haven't done it yet, set up some kind of "office" where you can direct your job search. Make this a place where you can take calls, handle correspondence, and keep track of your research and other information. A separate room (such as a spare bedroom) works best, but even a corner in the basement can help.

  You will need a desk, comfortable chair, phone, computer, Internet access, space to file materials/information, and space to work. It doesn't need to be fancy, but it does need to be comfortable and provide you with the privacy needed to direct your Plan for Action. When you are in this space, you are "at work."

- Maintain your normal schedule. Don't sleep late. Get dressed each morning just as if you were going to be out talking to people—because you probably will. One successful person with whom we worked sat down at his "office" every morning at 7:30, coffee in hand, and read the local and national newspapers, just as he had for 10 years prior. His reaction: "It really helped!"

- If you're not in some kind of physical-fitness program now, get yourself into one. Some people walk, some jog, some play golf or lift weights or dance or do other forms of exercise. The important thing is that you're doing something! Remember, exercise helps relieve stress and anxiety and enables you to think more clearly. Exercise also releases body chemicals that help keep depression away. If you're a bit overweight, the extra exercise can help reduce the pounds and simply help you feel better about yourself.

- Watch your diet and eat right. Eat balanced, reasonable-sized meals. Excessive coffee can increase tension and appetite. Excessive alcohol can dull your thinking ability (plus add weight). Excessive sweets and sugars can increase tension and irritability.

- View your activity as fulfilling your "job requirements," except now your job is to find a new position in another company as quickly as possible.

- Set weekly and daily goals in terms of contacts to make and research to conduct. Keep a record of your activity. People who devote four to eight hours to their job search per day become JobGetters faster than those who devote only a few hours each week. Take time on Mondays to set up these goals, and time on Friday to review your progress.

- Maintain your physical appearance. First impressions are important, and you will want to look good. For some this may mean investing in a new interviewing wardrobe. An investment in an interviewing wardrobe can often have a tremendous payback in terms of higher salary in the next position. If finances are a major concern, look for the recycled-clothing shops or job search "closets" that exist in many cities.

In the past several years, we have observed that candidates who are out on the streets meeting and talking with people are those who maintain their energy and confidence. On the other hand, those who sit back at home and merely mail out their resumes are often those who get discouraged. Sure, they'll eventually get hired. But the process is likely to drag on much longer than it needs to, and the position may be much less satisfying than it could be.

People who are out talking with other people are getting positive feedback, even though each contact does not yield either a job offer or an additional name of someone to see. The personal meetings and contacts provide feedback and candidates are affirmed in their ability to contribute to a new organization.

Those who sit back and merely mail out their resumes receive no direct feedback. Instead, their feedback comes from either receiving no response from their letters or from some form of a rejection letter. With each rejection letter, the body cringes and shrivels a little bit more.

However, every personal contact that at least yields an additional person on your side and on the lookout for openings for you is a confidence builder. And the way to turn job hunting into JobGetting is to make use of all the confidence builders you can get!

Others can be job hunters. That's their business. We want you to turn job hunting into JobGetting. And you can!

Use the Deems JobGetting Skills System; then savor the deep satisfaction of turning job hunting into JobGetting. Enjoy!

CARMEN'S STORY

"It works; if you follow the system, it works! It really does!" Carmen was ecstatic. "I just got the phone call I've been wanting, and it's all because of your system," she continued. Then Carmen went on to tell how, through her networking, she had found an opening for a call-center manager in an organization considered one of the best to work for in her city.

"Jorge told me about the opening," she continued, "and then he gave me the name of the person who would make the decision. And his phone number!" She researched the organization and learned as much as she could about it. Then she googled the key leaders of the company after reading their bios in the Investor Relations section of the Web site.

Carmen called the person directly, just as the system suggests. "He said I should call HR and I told him I could do that," Carmen added, "but when I said I didn't want to clutter up his desk with my paperwork if what he needed doing isn't what I do best, there was a pause. Then he asked me to tell him what it is I do best," Carmen added. "I knew he was interested from that point on."

Carmen continued to research the organization. She talked with several people about what it was like working in that organization, what the organization's plans were for the future, and what took extra time and energy from their leaders. Carmen also called the hiring manager again.

"I called the manager back again," Carmen added, "and this time I had some specific questions about the call-center operations. For example," she continued, "I had learned that the company wanted to hire more people just out of college. So I asked him about it and he reported their recruiting efforts weren't as successful as desired." Then she asked whether the company was sending out recruiters from among its Gen-Y employees. The answer was no.

"And then he asked me to tell him more about what I was thinking. The call turned from an interview into a discussion about recruiting top talent. It was exciting because I had a chance to tell him how I would go about solving some of their problems," Carmen added.

She knew she would be having a formal interview, so Carmen began to research what others had to say about being a call-center manager. Even though she never had that job, she knew how it could be done—and could be done better.

If you've read the chapter on interviewing and this chapter, then you know how the interview went. Carmen made sure to thank the three leaders who had conducted the interview (and had shown her around the building and introduced her to other managers). Before she left the interview, however, she paused and added, "I'm excited about working at ABC Corporation because of the way you treat your people," she began, "and I want the job!"

Carmen sent a thank-you note to each of three managers. The call came within two days of her interview.

"It works," she reported. "It really does!"

"When one door of happiness closes, another opens; but often we look so long at the closed door that we do not see the one that has been opened for us!"
—Helen Keller

CHAPTER 9

HOW DO I NEGOTIATE THE FINAL PACKAGE?

You've gone through the Job Loss Reaction Cycle. You've identified what you have to offer and polished how you present yourself. You've explored ways to find job openings. You developed and then implemented your Plan for Action. Now, an offer has been made. It matches what you do best and you want the job.

But the total package offered to you isn't quite what you had in mind. Now what?

When to Negotiate

The time to negotiate is only after a firm offer has been made—never before! Too many offers have not been made simply because a candidate tried to get some kind of special perk prior to the formal offer.

But can you negotiate the final package? Usually. There are some organizations whose first offer, other than for executive and senior-officer levels, is their best offer. This is often the case in organizations that have firm salary steps or pay grades. You'll find out about that, however, during your research of a company. Usually, but not always, organizations will tell you if there is no negotiation. With organizations that don't expect to negotiate, all you can do is consider the total package and then say yes or no.

Most companies, however, expect to negotiate the final package by at least 10 to 20 percent for professional and management-level positions. Public-sector positions such as government jobs, higher education, and so on, do not always have much negotiating space—but they might. Again, let your research guide you.

Each offer and situation is unique. Although the following does not apply to all situations, it does provide a framework from which you can develop your specific strategy and improve your preparedness to negotiate the final package.

If someone within the organization is part of your network, ask the person whether negotiating the final package is available.

Why Should I Negotiate?

There are four reasons to negotiate the final package:

- It is a sign of confidence and energy to negotiate, and people who do so (or even those who make a reasonable attempt to do so) will be considered a strong new team member.

- People who negotiate do so out of strength. They know what they have to offer and they know they will produce. That's the kind of employee a decision maker wants: someone who has the confidence to succeed.

- For any position, the company has invested a good amount of time and dollars in the selection process. They will not let a few dollars or some other perks keep them from their number-one choice. Unless your requests are out of line, the company will not pull their offer away.

- Decision makers do not enjoy rejection. They do not enjoy the prospect of someone turning them down because the job offer wasn't quite good enough. Unless the decision maker is for some reason prevented from doing so, a reasonable request on your part will not stand in the way of the decision maker getting his or her first choice.

How Do I Negotiate?

When the offer is made, either verbally or in writing, let them know you appreciate it, you're very interested, but you do need time to consider their offer or discuss it in detail with your family. At the senior level, several days (sometimes longer) to review the offer is typical. If they pressure you for an immediate decision, you might want to reconsider your own interest in working for the company. At the very least, indicate to them that you would be happy to let them know of your decision "first thing tomorrow morning."

Under only rare occasions should a person accept an offer on the spot. Instead, always ask for time: Next day. Two days later. After I've talked with my family. After all, you don't want to make a career decision that is akin to impulse buying.

Here is one way you can respond:

> *I appreciate the offer, and I'm excited about the challenges and opportunities here at XYZ Corporation. I need some time to discuss this in final detail*

*with my family. Is there a good time on Wednesday or Thursday that I can
get back in touch with you?*

This is a standard kind of response. The decision maker knows you are
interested, knows you want the position, and understands that you need some
time. The decision maker also understands that when you contact him or her
again, it will probably include asking for something additional.

Here's another approach:

> *I appreciate the offer, and I'm sure we can work out the final details. I can
> begin on the date you suggested, but the total salary package is lower than
> what I had expected. I need some time to talk this over with my family—
> can I get back to you sometime on Thursday?*

This kind of response clearly indicates that you're ready, but the salary isn't
right yet. Depending on the power of the decision maker you're talking with,
he or she may counter with a higher salary after your statement. The stronger
executive will usually counter with a higher salary on the spot and then pause
and wait for your reaction.

Our recommendation is that when a counter offer is immediately made, or
when it is clear to you that the offer is firm as it was given, you should still ask
for time to discuss the offer with family and indicate that you will be in touch
on a designated day or time.

How Much Should You Ask For?

Set your sights on a total compensation package that brings you a 10 to 20
percent increase over your previous compensation. You can always lower your
target if it is beyond reality or you have been unemployed for an extended
period and just need to get back to work. Just remember to think in terms of
total compensation. There can be a significant difference in pay and benefits
from one organization to another. Typically, the cash value of benefits is equal
to an average of 30 percent of your pay.

If the job offer would put you in a different geographic location, you need to
be realistic. A 30 percent increase to move from Kansas City to New York
City isn't any kind of real-income increase: In fact, your cost of living in that
move will bring a decrease in spendable dollars. Do your research! A number of
sources provide a cost-of-living comparison for major cities and globally. Use
the Internet to find out how the cost of living in the suggested new location
compares with the cost of living where you are now. You can find cost-of-living
calculators at www.salary.com, www.payscale.com, or www.careerperfect.com,
or many other good sites. You may find it helpful to compare calculator results
on more than one site.

If, however, the offer for the position is already 15 percent above the normal range for that kind of job in that city, you might want to focus on perks that do not cost the company in direct dollars, such as insurance coverage, a child care plan, fitness-center benefits, or added vacation time. This means that your research of the area and company must include the compensation for comparable people and responsibilities.

If accepting the position means a relocation for you, moving expenses or bonuses will also be part of your negotiation. Relocation assistance varies from company to company. Do your research and find out what is typical within that industry. Consider what kind of moving assistance will be provided: Will they help with finding and purchasing a new home, and provide living expenses until that new home is found? Some companies also offer to purchase your old house as a way to help speed up the process.

Make a Counteroffer

Make your counteroffer at the designated time. Show your enthusiasm for the offer, the company, and the decision makers:

> *The opportunity to be part of XYZ Corporation is exciting, but as I review the total package, it seems that the cash salary is somewhat low. My research for this level position in this city is $A to $B. Because of my experience, I was thinking more in terms of $XX,XXX (or full health coverage, etc.). And if we can get close to that figure, we can finalize a starting date.*

Your counteroffer is not a threat but a request for consideration, made in such a way that the decision maker knows that a little bit of movement on his or her side will enable you to begin work with a lot of enthusiasm.

If you do your research and uncover what the salary range in that city is for a similar position, you can place yourself within that range. What's important is that the decision makers know you have researched the city and the position and you know the salary range for similar positions.

Continue Negotiating

Continue your negotiations until you think that is all you can negotiate, or until you get the perks that are important. You must be cautious at this point, however, that your counteroffers are not so ambitious that you scare the decision maker or make him or her begin to question the wisdom of the initial offer.

Often you can negotiate some of the smaller perks after you accept the offer and then during informal discussion about your plans to begin work. Try casually saying something like, "You know, membership in CCC Association would certainly be advantageous."

Accept the Offer

Enthusiastically accept the negotiated offer, and let the decision maker know that you appreciate the extra perks that have become part of the total package. Show your energy and enthusiasm for the new position as you finalize your beginning date, and then be in touch prior to that date with questions or comments that show you have already begun to work.

If you can, get written confirmation of the offer. Some companies will offer this before you have time to ask. If such a letter is not offered, you can ask for a letter of agreement. Decision makers will understand and will typically comply with your request.

Here's to your continued successes!

FELICIA'S STORY

When Felicia got the call about her offer, she was ecstatic. "The claims manager's spot is exactly what I wanted," she said. "But." The salary was lower than she expected and the new company's policy would cut her vacation time down to two weeks from four. She started to set her strategy.

"I contacted the person I'd report to," Felicia added, "and said I was really excited about the opportunity but needed a couple of days to think about it." They agreed that Felicia would meet the department manager who offered her the job and the SVP of operations in two days. Then she went to work doing her research.

Felicia knew that the company sometimes negotiated final agreements. And she had talked with two people inside the organization who had negotiated their final offers. She was determined to do the same.

In looking over her notes, she remembered two former co-workers who were now with two different companies. She contacted each and asked them to find out the salary range for claims managers within their organizations. Next she got on the Internet and typed "claims managers salaries" into a search engine. Some of the listed sites were helpful, and some were not. The two former co-workers were the most helpful. People already doing what you want to be doing are usually your best source of reliable information.

(continued)

(continued)

Felicia was ready. After greeting the manager and SVP, she began: "I'm really excited about being a member of your organization! From what I've learned, you are one of the premier places to work in this city and I'm looking forward to being part of it. The salary and vacation package isn't quite what I was looking for, however. Doing my research on this city, I found the income range for claims managers is from $A to $B. Given my experience I believe I belong near the top of that range, and if you could bump up the salary by about $X, we can talk in detail about start date."

Felicia had indicated her enthusiasm about being part of the organization. She showed that she knew, from her own research, what other claims managers were making in that city. She also stated that she was ready to go to work, if....

There was a pause in the conversation. After a moment or two, the person who would be her manager smiled and said, "I think we can accommodate that." Then Felicia continued.

"There's one more thing," Felicia continued. Then she told how her family had planned a two-week vacation for the fall. Location and dates had been set and deposits sent in. "I'd really like to be able to keep that trip," Felicia continued, "even though it comes within the first three months of being on the job. We have also become used to four weeks of vacation annually. How can we make this work?"

The three talked about vacations and families and shared experiences. Finally her new boss added, "It's not the usual," he began, "but I think we can accommodate it. I think it's important that we maintain our company's policy of being family-friendly." Felicia ended up with the fall vacation already planned and negotiated three weeks of vacation time for her first year with the new company. It was a done deal.

The basic principle is that most organizations expect to negotiate. If they don't, they will tell you. As long as your counter is within reason, it is most often accepted or the company counters again. And then the discussion continues until an agreement is reached. After all the time (and money) the company has spent in recruiting, interviewing, and selecting you, a few dollars or a few days isn't going to make them take back the offer.

"If you think you can or if you think you can't...either way you're right!"
—Henry Ford

CHAPTER 10

HOW DO I GET STARTED IN MY NEW JOB?

You have your new job and you are excited about the new challenges and new opportunities. Now, what do you do to make the most of this new opportunity? This chapter gives our advice for starting off on the right foot and building career success that lasts.

Getting Started

Your new role probably involves something similar to what you've done before, so it will not be totally new. What will be new are the people you will be working with and the company culture.

Your first few days may consist of many highs and lows. The highs often come from the excitement of the position or your own pleasure in tackling the new challenges. You feel energized and ready to take on whatever comes at you. The lows may be a sense of frustration at yourself for not learning new things as quickly as you would like, or a feeling of being "out of the loop" as you see your new co-workers enjoying a familiarity with each other that you don't feel—*yet*. These lows may make you feel down at times or hesitant in what you do.

NOTE: If you haven't already, now is the time to write to your network of people who have assisted you during this transition, thank them once again, and let them know of your new position.

Several activities will help to stabilize these highs and lows by enabling you to get to know the company culture, your new supervisor, and the people you'll be working with:

- **Get acquainted with your new boss.** Find out what she or he considers to be the high-priority tasks. Make sure you know what is expected of you and how the results of your work will be evaluated. If it isn't offered, you may want to ask for some special time, such as a lunch, to discuss some of these issues in more detail. This is all part of getting acquainted.

- **Don't try to make people do things "your way."** Stop yourself from saying, "Well, at ABC Corporation we did it this way." Nothing will turn off new peers, superiors, and subordinates more quickly than to refer to how you used to do things. If you do believe that a strategy you're familiar with from a previous position is more effective, you can say, "Have you considered this approach?" Maybe they tried it and it didn't work, for reasons you're not familiar with yet. Or maybe it is a new approach for them. Either way, they will appreciate not being compared to your previous employer.

- **Ask questions in a non-threatening way.** Develop a style of asking non-question questions, or questions that do not end with a question mark. This approach to finding information is less threatening than to ask a specific question, and will convey that you are a good team player. Here are several ways to begin questions that do not end in a question mark:

  It would help me if I knew....

  I need to know...and it would be helpful if you could explain this to me....

  That statement is not clear to me, and it would help if you could explain it further....

- **Show your enthusiasm and energy for the company.** Get to work ahead of time and don't be in a hurry to leave at the end of the day. Take an extra minute or two to chat with co-workers or simply to say "See you tomorrow." Some days it pays to be the last to leave.

- **Be willing to take on extra tasks as appropriate.** There is always more to do than there is time, and being willing to take on extra tasks shows your enthusiasm for the new position and organization. It may take extra time and energy, but it will be noted by others. You'll gain a reputation as someone who is enthusiastic about their work.

- **Take time to get to know your peers and people who report to you.** One way to keep relations positive is to ask people for their input—and then take it seriously.

- **Adopt the mindset of an external consultant.** Constantly ask yourself the question external consultants ask: "What needs doing that isn't being done or could be done better?" When you see things that could be improved, develop a preliminary plan and present it to your superior. Or take it to a couple of your peers or employees and ask for their reactions and input. At least while you're still new, it is generally best *not* to jump right into "improving" things on your own (unless, of course, you were specifically hired to do just that; if that is the case, it is still helpful to get input from others).

- **Know that you will make friends at your new job.** Remember that your best friends were once total strangers. You will find new friends in your new organization.

Preparing for Your Future

As you begin your new job, you can also continue the work you started in shaping and preparing your career future. A good way to do this is to begin developing your own personal career development plan. Many companies have each of their employees develop an annual professional development plan, so go ahead and take the initiative. It shows extra energy and enthusiasm and will be a valuable tool further down the road.

Focus on the areas you want to strengthen or simply to know more about. Identify the seminars and conferences or other learning opportunities that will help you further develop your own expertise. Take advantage of any development opportunities or tuition assistance your new employer offers. Set your goals and design your strategy to meet those goals. An employee who is continually looking for ways to learn more and improve performance is a valued employee.

A study by the American Society for Training and Development identified 16 basic workplace skills and divided them into seven groups:

1. Knowing How to Learn
2. Reading, Writing, and Computation Skills
3. Listening and Speaking
4. Creative Thinking and Problem Solving
5. Self-Esteem, Goal Setting/Motivation, and Career Development
6. Interpersonal Skills, Negotiation, and Teamwork
7. Organizational Effectiveness and Leadership

One way to develop your own personal career development plan is to use these seven areas as your plan's outline. Then you can design how you intend to develop yourself in each of these seven areas.

Keeping Track of Your Results

After all the work you did to land this job, you now understand the importance of knowing the results of your work. Now you can set up a new file to keep a record of your results. Once a month, or at least once a quarter, review what you have done in the previous time period and make your notes.

This is the best time to quantify those results because the events will be fresh in your mind. Also, necessary data is more accessible in case you have to generate some information to quantify those results. You can include your new results in a written or verbal report to your new boss, which may be helpful during performance reviews. If the project you worked on increased profits or decreased costs, make sure your boss knows about it, as well as your own role and the role of co-workers in the project's success.

In fact, morale for all employees can be improved by seeing reminders of the results of the good work they do. There are lots of ways to do this, such as to create posters or other types of announcements to indicate the results of the department's work. It doesn't have to be big or fancy—just something that everyone can see and that reminds them that their work does make a difference.

JOSE'S STORY

Jose was part of a layoff and worked hard at JobGetting. He got the job he really wanted: supervising a team of eight professionals in the marketing unit of a fast-growing company. His first day was spent meeting people and beginning to get acquainted. He met with his boss and the two discussed Jose's challenges for the next year. He met with the people on his team. He met with other supervisors in the marketing department and scheduled a meeting with the research and development director—a person he would be working with very closely.

The second day, Jose called his team around him at about 8:15 a.m. As they stood, he asked the group to take a couple of minutes to talk about what each person was doing, what roadblocks they were running into, and what would help that person be more effective. The conversation was quick, taking no more than 15 minutes.

Then he asked whether the group would like to have this kind of huddle every morning. It was a unanimous yes. "We didn't always know who was doing what before," one team member stated. "This keeps us posted—besides, I can always use the insight from others on our team."

Jose continued to meet with other key people within the company, particularly those who were impacted by his department. There were scheduled lunches, meetings, and breakfasts.

When the team's plan for rolling out a new product was completed two weeks ahead of schedule and under budget, Jose made a small poster and placed it where every team member could see: "Congratulations for Being Ahead of Schedule and Under Budget on the Rollout Project. Great Work, Team!" The team liked it. Employees from other units saw the poster and commented to the team about it. Even the CEO came by and said "Thanks!"

At the end of his first month in the new job, Jose sat down at his desk and put a label on a file folder: "Results." Then he made some notes on the things that the team had accomplished in the past several weeks. For each item, he tried to quantify the results as closely as possible. To quantify one result, he realized he needed to talk to someone in sales. He made a note to himself to schedule that meeting.

Then Jose leaned back in his chair, looked around him as his team worked, and smiled. He made a note to himself to call his old boss at his old company to tell him "thank you."

"Don't wait for your ship to come in...swim out to it!"
—Anonymous

But I Don't Feel Like It!

We know what you mean. There are days when you just don't feel like getting up, or getting dressed for an interview, or knocking on doors, or making phone calls, or sitting down at your computer, or any of those things that turn job hunting into JobGetting.

Sometimes you just need to take a few days off. That's okay. But don't let a few days turn into a few weeks. We've seen it happen. That's when people are really feeling sorry for themselves. There's a lot of self-pity (sniveling, we call it).

Real Stories

You don't have time for sniveling. There are things to do, and calls to make, and people to see, and letters to write, and contacts to make. A few hours, okay. A day or two, okay. If it lasts more than a day or two, you need to take action. It may help to think about how some other people have made things work.

Richard

Richard was on the staff at a major Illinois university when he lost his job. He was informed in July and the job ended December 31. Of course he didn't begin his job search until November. Not real swift.

And then he focused on only one application at a time. He didn't always network very well, but he did make phone calls to companies that placed ads that were of interest. It took him until the next September (that's nine months) to finalize something. He came in second for two good positions, but never got an offer. There were down days. But he kept at it. Now Richard is one of the nation's leading experts on the JobGetting skills process, and recognized as an innovator in designing strategies to help people make change work. He's the author of 12 books, with more in the works. The key: He kept at it even when he didn't feel like it.

Morrie

Morrie worked the job search process for nearly a year before anything of real interest turned up. He talked with headhunters and venture-capital people, sent blind letters, and networked every day. He turned down two offers. "They didn't come close to what I was looking for," he reported. To maintain his energy, Morrie began jogging in the morning and walking with his wife in the evenings.

Fortunately, he had the financial resources to be somewhat selective. Finally, after ten months, three opportunities began to develop—all at once. "You told me it could happen like this," Morrie reported. "It was real tough," Morrie added, "and there were days I didn't want to do anything—but I did, anyway." Morrie is now a company leader for a small and growing special food-processing manufacturer.

Kelsey Grammer

Kelsey Grammer (TV's *Frasier*) has had one of the most bizarre lives. His father was murdered when Kelsey was 13, his sister murdered when he was 18, and his half-brothers killed in a shark attack when he was 25. He has been arrested for drug and alcohol abuse and has done time. "The best thing about life," he told a reporter, "is you can change, you can fix things, you can make amends.... The stuff that happens to you," he continued, "the traffic of life, does shape us but it doesn't have to define us."

Kelsey continues, "I believe that your duty is to prevail, to overcome your inheritance and your environment and do something a bit beyond what you were given."

Terri

Terri thought she had it made as public relations/marketing manager for a nonprofit professional association. Wrong. "When I was terminated," she explains, "it was like a bad dream. This wasn't the way it was supposed to work out." She took it hard. There were lots of days that she just didn't feel like doing anything. But she kept at it.

Terri began to analyze what she most enjoyed doing, and realized it was working with people and helping them through tough times. Now finished with her Ph.D., her emphasis is on how people go through growth and change, and how companies restrict or enhance these processes. She persevered.

Harold

Harold got caught in some internal politics and lost his job. He worked the JobGetting system hard and in five months had a new position in Kansas City with a VP title, more money, and more decision-making in a young, growing company. Several months later the company went under, and Harold was out looking again.

He found another position in Kansas City, but not at quite the same level. The pay was less and there was no officer title. "But I'm doing what I'm good at and what I enjoy," Harold reported. Two months later he was caught in a downsizing.

"That third time was so tough," Harold reported, "but I wasn't going to crash and burn. Others could, but I refused. Each day I'd get up early and run," he reported, "and I kept increasing my miles. It made the difference. The routine gave me the energy each day to make the calls, to be out talking to people." Now Harold is with a stable company in Cincinnati. The new company paid for his move, bought his old house, financed his new one, and "they're excited that I'm part of the management team."

He kept at it.

Sheryl

Sheryl anticipated the downsizing, "but I still wasn't ready for it when it included me," she reported. "It caught the family at a time when we were making some major decisions, and my husband was already going through a major career change."

She wondered what others in her field would think—after all, she had a national reputation and was considered by others as a major player in her area of expertise. "It was tough making those networking calls," Sheryl stated, "but I did—until someone suggested I take what I know and go to work for myself."

She pulled together a team of former co-workers and, armed with lots of energy, began a new company. Sheryl's reputation has been enhanced, the company is growing, and the team enjoys working together. "What more could you ask for?" (Yes, they're making money, too.)

No Sniveling!

Sure, you can have your down days (because you will), and there will be frustration at having to learn how to turn job hunting into JobGetting. For some, the whole process can be intimidating and difficult. But feeling sorry for yourself? You don't have time for it!

You need to resolve that you will get through it, learn from it, and grow from it. Here are three things you can do when you really feel down:

1. **Exercise.** Ride a bike, walk, jog, run, lift weights, play tennis, play handball, dance—do whatever you do to exercise. Keep at it until you feel better. It takes at least 20 minutes of exercise before those feel-good chemicals begin to be released in our bodies. Let those endorphins work for you. (Oh yes, be sure to get a physical exam before you begin any strenuous exercise program.)

2. **Review your resume.** Take time to read your resume from time to time. Focus on the achievements and accomplishments of your past. Affirm that you have many future contributions to make to many different organizations. Reading your resume should result in a very positive feeling about what you can do and what you can contribute to a new organization.

3. **Avoid the negative people.** We don't mean you should just stay inside all the time, but let's face it: There are some people who are always negative. Nothing goes right. Nobody does what they're supposed to. Even the sun doesn't come up in the right place. Our advice: Avoid them. You don't need their negativity. And too often, just being around them for five minutes puts a downer on your day. If they try to drag you into their negativity, tell them firmly, "I'm sorry, but I don't have time to complain about.... I have too many other things to do." Stick with your friends who are your cheerleaders.

The key is to keep going—even when you don't feel like it!

Remember, there is so much to be done...and you have so much to contribute!

"The traffic of life shapes us...but it doesn't have to define us!"
—Kelsey Grammer

SHOULD I BECOME SELF-EMPLOYED?

Self-employment is increasingly an option for people. Whether it involves buying a company, buying into a company, or starting up a new company or freelance venture, it's one way for people to focus on what they most enjoy doing—and staying in control. Being self-employed works for some and doesn't for others.

Here are some real-life stories of people we know who made the transition:

- **George** was a bank manager before his job loss. After several months of job searching, he responded to a request to help prepare a company's loan application. Before long George was too busy acting as a financial consultant to corporations to worry about a job search. Teaming up with a friend, he opened a consulting company dealing with corporate financial problems.

- **Jennie** was a marketing specialist in an international company. She spent a good deal of time working directly with foreign governments. After her job loss, it took her only three weeks to form her own consulting company. Now she helps U.S. companies expand their operations into foreign countries. She is still working directly with other governments and making 50 percent more than when she worked for someone else.

- **Sheryl** was a culinary book editor who, after 20 years, was reorganized out. She enjoyed her work; did it very well; and had a good reputation as a food expert, writer, and editor. After talking with several decision makers from large food product companies, Sheryl joined with two other displaced workers and formed a new communications company. The group was profitable after one year and, after only three years, gained national recognition for their ability to produce high-quality custom print and video products.

- **Bill** was a bank executive who had worked for one bank since the day he graduated from high school. After 31 years, he was out. As an operations manager, Bill knew how to manage people and processes. He enjoyed it, did it well, and preferred to stay in some kind of similar position. After talking with a business broker, he met another person who was also considering investing in a business. Together the two bought a business they considered had a future, made some changes to reduce overhead while expanding customer service, and began growing the company. "The numbers are even better than we had anticipated," Bill reported.

- **Nancy** was good at organizing special events such as social gatherings, fund-raisers, and public relations programs. Given the chance to elect early retirement, she did—and within two weeks she became the city's first and only professional event organizer. With an office in her home, she's making what she calls a "livable income." More important, Nancy reported, she is doing what she most enjoys doing.

Self-Employment Issues

No, not all issues are dollar issues. But dollars do figure in very prominently. If you're thinking about self-employment, here are several issues to consider:

- **A job is an unmet need.** Sounds obvious, but we often forget the truth. If there are no unmet needs, there are no jobs. So start looking for things that need doing that aren't being done or could be done better. When you find a match between an unmet need and what you most enjoy doing, there is the possibility of becoming self-employed.

- **What do I have to offer?** You need to be clear about how you can meet an unmet need. What do your potential customers need? And can you meet that specific need? The more clearly you can describe what you have to offer, the greater the probability of your success.

- **Do I have the strengths and instincts to work for myself?** It takes a lot of drive and initiative to go into business for yourself. Do you have the drive and ego-strength to be on your own? Maybe you have some of the desire, but you need a partner to help add balance to your own strengths. It's okay if you believe you need a partner to add balance. That's just good thinking!

- **Is there a market for what I have to offer?** Do some market research before you reach your final decision. If there isn't a market for what you want to do (unmet needs), and you can't create a market, there's no sense in pursuing that idea any further.

- **Will my family support my self-employment?** Support from your spouse is essential, and if your spouse or significant other opposes your self-employment you may want to reconsider. Other family members can help by giving their personal support and encouragement.

- **Do I have access to the needed resources?** Resources include financial, but they also include advice and guidance in preparing a business plan, developing a marketing strategy, handling inventory, and so on. There are a number of resources available, such as the Small Business Development Center (SBDC) network (part of the Small Business Administration) and programs offered by community colleges. To be successful, you need to be ready to learn from those who've learned the hard way.

Resources

A number of resources are available to help you think through what it takes to become successfully self-employed. One of the first places to stop is the Small Business Administration's office nearest your home (locate it at www.sba.gov/aboutsba/sbaprograms/sbdc/sbdclocator/index.html). Talk with one of their specialists. Ask for information about their introductory workshop (often conducted at a community college) on how to start your own business.

Most states have some form of the Small Business Development Center (SBDC) network. Check it out. They specialize in helping individuals seriously study whether to go into business for themselves.

People who are already self-employed are another great resource. They already are where you are considering going. They know what has worked for them and what hasn't. And they can help you keep from making mistakes. Take time for some information gathering. Meet with several who have gone into business for themselves and be ready with your questions, such as the following:

- What do you like best?
- What do you like least?
- What would you do differently?
- What advice can you give me?

Some of your best information will come from those who have made the jump themselves. Most will be willing to give you time and be very honest in what they have to report. But unless you personally know someone who is already doing what you are thinking about doing, don't bother to talk with potential competitors. You might be, after all, future significant competition.

This is not a book on becoming self-employed. We mention it because for some people it is a viable option, especially when jobs are hard to come by. It may be their best option. Our own suggestion, after going from a company around a kitchen table to an organization with offices in several states, is this: Do your research before you jump.

ACTION WORDS

Here is a list of action words you can use to begin your resume one-liners. When you begin each statement with an action word, the reader begins to realize that you are a person who gets things done.

Other lists of action words are available on the Internet, such as www. jobweb.com/resumesample.aspx?id=280 (a nice list) or www.quintcareers.com/ action_skills.html (another good list, divided by skills categories).

Accomplished	Demonstrated	Increased
Achieved	Designed	Initiated
Addressed	Developed	Installed
Analyzed	Devised	Instituted
Appointed	Directed	Introduced
Approved	Doubled	Invented
Balanced	Earned	Launched
Completed	Edited	Led
Conceived	Elected	Maintained
Conducted	Eliminated	Managed
Consolidated	Established	Monitored
Constructed	Expanded	Negotiated
Controlled	Financed	Obtained
Converted	Founded	Operated
Coordinated	Generated	Organized
Created	Hired	Originated
Decreased	Improved	Performed
Delivered	Improvised	Planned

Prepared	Revised	Traded
Prevented	Scheduled	Trained
Processed	Serviced	Transferred
Produced	Simplified	Transformed
Promoted	Sold	Translated
Proposed	Solved	Trimmed
Provided	Staffed	Tripled
Purchased	Started	Uncovered
Recommended	Streamlined	Unified
Redesigned	Strengthened	Utilized
Reduced	Structured	Vacated
Reorganized	Succeeded	Verified
Researched	Supervised	Widened
Resolved	Traced	Withdrew
Reviewed	Tracked	Won

INDEX

J

X–Z

NOTES

NOTES